# CLOUD COMPUTING ESSENTIALS

**BIBHUTI MOHANTY**

Made with ♥ on the Notion Press Platform
www.notionpress.com

# Contents

# Part I

# CHAPTER ONE

# INTRODUCTION TO CLOUD COMPUTING

---

We need not worry where and what the computing power is. Just consume it from anywhere. Don't worry about the actors behind.

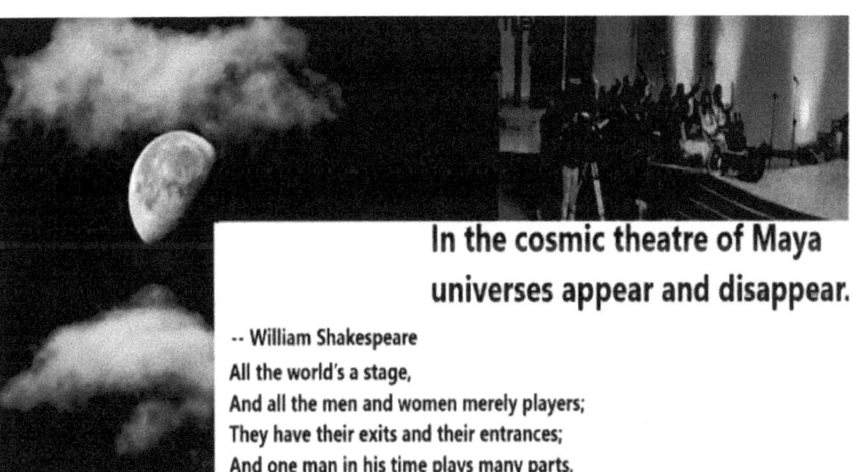


This short book aims at laying a broad cloud framework for cloud engineers and architects. While it is not possible to cover each cloud at depth, sufficient care has been taken to bring to light the major services from major cloud providers and to highlight the challenges in success in cloud. From devops to ERP all service fronts of corporates are moving to cloud. User is no more aware from which cloud or on-prem data centres the data is coming. The data sources and engines to crunch the data are spread across the globe and edge & mobile computing coupled with advances in AI make the data and content delivery fast and insightful. Internet is heavily utilised as never before as one single network platform providing resources and information for individual to large global corporates.

It covers some key services from ibm, azure, aws and google cloud. It provides some real life migration use cases on how to migrate to cloud. It provides some examples of how different cloud services are leveraged from a typical service unit of a corporate. It provides some example layout of cloud enabled corporate in terms of networking. It also gives an example of terraform based provisiong of a OCP cluster hihlighting the degree of automation possible in devops practices. It also answers some fundamental questions which can be handy for students and professionals seeking career in cloud.

The expectation from cloud computing has increased manifold over years. Today, cloud consumers from individual to big corporates expect cloud to be highly cost effective, manageable, available and secure. This short book tries to fathom many critical and potential issues with cloud journey so that cloud experience is smooth and modernization drives are hassle free. Some use cases are cited as reference for cloud practioners. While material on cloud is overflowing on internet crucial and concise information on cloud is missing. It doesn't just answers some cloud adoption challenges but show some consumption cases for getting started in the cloud journey.

There is a section on Cloud native framework & kubernetes.
It is never a good practice to move to cloud without a planned migration.

Q: Where are all going? What is so special there?
Ans: Cloud
Q: Are we ready?
Ans: Don't know.
Q: Lets go there first. We will adjust there later.

What is Cloud Computing?

It is an on-demand availability of computing resources when user needs them for providing services. It is a globally accessible offerings of compute, storage, network and application resources with self-service facility. Consumers both corporate and individuals can quickly provision, integrate & consume various kinds of software and hardware resources from anywhere suiting their application needs from more than one cloud providers. It is cost effective based on metered usage. Global mobile and multi media networks complement and supplement adoption of cloud computing. Corporate can go with hybrid models with combination of private cloud and public cloud meeting their security and business needs. Resources on cloud can be scaled up and down, & deprovisioned quickly thus consumption and billing is optimal. Resources can be quickly purchased on a pay-as-you-go basis, so there is no need for massive up-front spending thus new business setup & modernization drives can be expedited by adoption of cloud. Managing, auditing & monitoring can be provided by cloud service providers as consumable services thus bridging the skill gaps to manage the cloud resources. High availability and Disaster management capability can be quickly setup & tested on cloud.

In cloud all services are available under one umbrella.

Many processes like management, disaster recovery, operations, costing etc.    change.

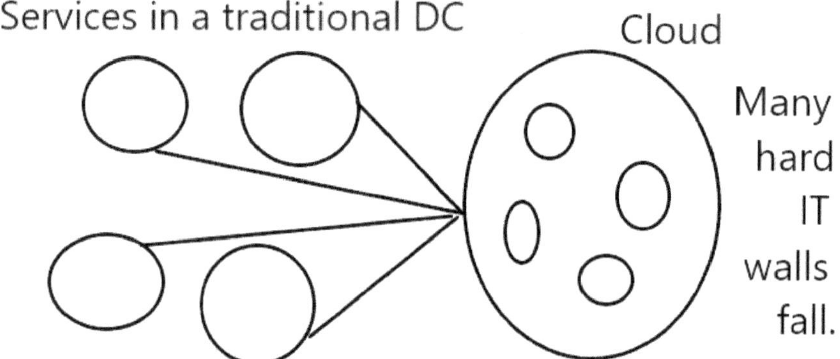


All services (computing, network, storage, middlewares etc.) of customer data centres converge on cloud when migrated.
Many teams and service units converge under one umbrella. Work culture changes too.

Why Cloud Computing is so essential and what are the challenges in adopting it?

Modernization of IT companies is largely driven by adoption of cloud platforms. Cloud platforms have evolved in a big way. Cloud platforms apart from providing tools and processes for on-prem to cloud migration have diversified into various critical services which are essential for all IT companies. Cloud deployment and management models have undergone a sea change. Open source software adoptions with cloud marketplaces, utilization of cloud native services, use of kubernetes & virtualization platforms are all now easily realizable on almost all major cloud platforms.

With maturing of hybrid and multi cloud delivery & deployment models, the foot prints of IT companies are now truely global.

Apart from reduction of cost, other aspects of cloud like ease of development, deployment, & maintenance has made Devops and DevSecops practices really realizable. SRE (Software Reliability Engineering) has matured with different monitoring, logging, troubleshooting, auditing, security & dashboard services.

With cloud platforms managing the IT resources in a performing, secure & cost effective manner, IT executives have now enough bandwidth to focus on customer satisfaction. In other words, IT enablement has reached the last mile. With "pay as you go" costing models & auto-scaling features, massive upfront investments is no more a deterrent for several research projects with no clear bounded timelines and resource consumptions.

The initial inhibition in adopting cloud is gone. Cloud platforms have helped Start-ups in a big big way. Availability of man power with cloud skills is no more a challenge. In fact, economic feasibility, choice of software components, flexibility & manageability have largely improved with cloud adpotion. The fear of vendor lock-in has lessened.

Major virtualization and containerization platforms or solutions are now available on the cloud horizon. For example, in ibm cloud you can find VMware Foundation services which can be used to build VMware workloads that integrate with other cloud native services. ARO or Azure Redhat Openshift is a K8s platform from Redhat which is now available in azure cloud as a managed solution for building containerised or microservice based applications on cloud.

There are different types of cloud. Public cloud is accessible over internet. Private cloud is accessible over a private network. Hybrid cloud is a combination of cloud and On-prem data centers. Multi cloud is combination of more than one cloud. Depending on the requirement an organization builds its cloud presence in various deployment models suiting.

Cloud market places are rich in different types of open source products and services which can be utilised for modernization. The major challenge in adopting cloud lies with arriving at an accurate analysis of the current business in terms of cost, security, manageability, application needs, delivery SLAs, scalability, flexibility, high availability, DR capabilities, current vendor agreements, current licenses etc. It is not an easy task for a large corporate with complex business processes. The type & size of data coupled with integration challenges requires a careful evaluation of matching cloud services and migration mechanisms. Cloud migration tools and services offered by cloud vendors vary in scope. Several PoC needs to be conducted with some typical data sizes in terms of speed of data transfer, security of data transfer, accuracy of data transfer and cost of data transfer. The type & no of workloads like vm, baremetal, database, web server, load balancer, dns server, AD server, router, firewall, gateway, applications etc. really matters in terms of approach to migration. Duration and number of cycles of migration really matters when inter application integration requires closely coupled sub systems to be migrated in one go, otherwise complex network setup may be needed to allow business continuity. Imagine a case when one subsystem is in cloud and another closely coupled sub system is still on-prem and due to issue in getting proper down time windows cutover is challenging. A migration task force needs to be created to assess the data migration needs. While one team is doing PoC on cloud, another team may be doing data discovery.

**Automation is everywhere.** All top automation tools & practices like AI, Ansible, IaC, Devops converge in cloud. Massive job cuts are expected down the line. Competion is fierce. Yesterday's giants are sometimes nowhere. Journey of Idea to executions is shortened. A new online work culture has changed the lifestyles of millions of professionals. Internet is ripe and is in use everywhere in every segments of life. Mobility of workforce and resources combine as never before. Open source adoption has challenged survivals of many products and services. Social media data is used for marketing, election campaign & Inventory optimization. Everyone is under scanner of IoT devices. Pace of IT revolution has increased and there is no room for laziness. Workplaces are utilized 24/7. Workforces are available globally 24/7 in shifts. Businessman can get trends in market with press of a button or even asking a few words to a device. Yes, this Computing evolution has touched common man's lives in big big way. It has both positive and negative sides.

**Which Cloud to choose?** You can go through some customer reviews on Gartner to find a matching solution based on many criteras like company size, industry and region. You also can filter on the basis of government or private sectors. You can have a several brain storming sessions within the corporate first before engaging with cloud providers' sales teams. Initial analysis of current pain points in product or service delivery & future goals is important before assessing different clouds. The goal whether short term or long term also plays a crucial role in cloud selection. Modernization of existing workloads can start in current state long before the migration happens providing a staregic path to cloud migration. Although many clouds provide IaaS, PaaS, SaaS & FaaS etc. existing solutions or services can better integrate with certain solutions of certain clouds. Finding the close match involves several rounds of detailed discussions with teams from business, operations, infrastructure, application, customers & sales. The intitial excitation to go to cloud should be supported & sustained by proper analysis and planning. Product migration and service migration may require different migration approaches. Some clouds you can choose for are GCP, Microsoft Azure, IBM Cloud, AWS, Oracle Cloud Infrastructure, Alibaba Cloud, Huawei Cloud SAP S/4HANA Implementation, and VMware Cloud.

Computing has evolved through many models like Distributed Systems, Mainframe Computing, Cluster Computing, Grid Computing, Virtualization, Web 2.0, Service Orientation and Utility Computing etc.

## Modernization

(**Source:** Cloud & K8s with Case Studies - Adoption Of Kubernetes Into Enterprise IT Strategy)

It is an ongoing activity in almost all IT organisations to remain competitive in terms of value generation by leveraging it services. Availability, Cost, operational flexibility, manageability, performance etc. are major drivers for modernisation.

Before cloud and containerisation modernisation primarily relied on hardware, firmware, software, apps, integration enhancement initiatives using hardware and software refresh cycles. Old equipment's were getting replaced with new equipment's generally included liasioning with OEM, ISV, Vendors, third parties, licence management etc. Horizontal scalability vs vertical scalability.

With cloud, containerisation, DevOps and AI modernization scope is very vast and several new key people and processes are introduced to successfully modernise the infra and apps. Anyway, migration and transformation are the two major processes or programs undertaken by enterprises on the journey to speed to market.

## Migration

Migration is cloud migration with or without containerisation. Migration methodology varies depending on type of workloads, spread of workloads, size of workloads and whether workloads are migrated to public cloud, private cloud, hybrid cloud or hybrid multi cloud.

Post vendor selection decision and scope definition, cloud migration generally starts with asset discovery in current DC followed by defining and assessing the tools along with laying out the migration roadmap. Several options and tools come into picture depending on the cloud deployment model, consumption model and operation models.

**Some tools from AWS**

AWS Migration Hub

Application Discovery Service

Database Migration Service

Server Migration Service

AWS Transfer for SFTP

Snowball

DataSync

IBM Cloud, Microsoft Azure, Google Cloud Platform etc. provide many migration tools and services.

## Transformation

Workloads migration may be migrated as is or are transformed as well along with migration. Example: Some physical servers may be virtualized and/or containerised. New service management offerings are integrated as well.

Several databases may change their models as part of the migration. New vendors and partners are introduced and there may be changes in how the new services post migration are managed and who manages. In fact, many factors like security in cloud environment, audit and compliance requirements and integration requirements make the exercises quite complex at times.

MTA and cloud-native apps are new buzz words in enterprises who pursue aggressive approach to reduce cost and add flexibility in IT operations.

In migration critical DBs are multi terabytes in size using oracle RAC & ASM.RAC is active active clustering unlike active passive OS clusters and powerful cluster storages are required to provide concurrent active/active r/w access from multiple nodes of the cluster. No of nodes in some clusters can be high and workloads deployed can be combination of OLAP and OLTP and there can be unpredictable IO bursts.

Sizing block sizes and assessing IOPS both at DB and OS level is tough. And architects struggle irrespective of many benchmarking tools. ASM is a powerful clustered filesystem from oracle that sits on top of a clustered storage.

Major cloud vendors provide options for granular IOPS based block storage provisioning with burst IO capabilities. Irrespective of all many offerings still the installations can fall short of requirement of highly concurrent 24/7 apps.

Storages offered by vendors can be raw, block, file, object etc. and involving SAN, VSAN, NAS, DAS, S3 based etc. Still migrations to public cloud can be a daunting task. Some Cloud migration tools on IBM Cloud like **HCX, Actifio, Zerto** etc. are worth trying. One more tool from Google called **velostrata** can be tested as well.

Actifio uses **incrementally updated image copies** (a powerful backup mechanism from oracle) to migrate super large oracle databases to cloud.

Container based migration is coming into picture in hybrid multi cloud environments. DBs are no more a concern for statefulset or stateful apps implementations after robust persistence storage implementations. Redhat OpeShift container platform integrates with major cloud vendors' storages. With adoption of SDN, SDDC etc. the migration projects are more and more challenging and exciting.

**Go serverless** way, go Kubernetes way. Decouple developers from servers and help them focus on solving business need. Cost and flexibility both can combine.

# CHAPTER TWO

# AWS

AWS or Amazon web services offers services in areas like Analytics, Application Integration, Compute, Billing, Containers and K8s, Databases, Developer Tools, IAM, IoT, Management and Governance, Migration Hub, ML, Networking, Route 53 DNS Service, Security, Storage and VMware Cloud on AWS.

Some useful services in analytics area are amazon redshift data warehouse, athena, amazon data firehose, data pipeline, EMR (managed hadoop framework), AWS Glue (a serverless data integration service), kinesis (real-time streaming data) and aws lake formation. In application integration some services are Simple Queue Service (a managed message queues), managed Apache Airflow, Simple notification service (managed message topics for pub/sub), Step functions etc. AWS compute service offering is truely rich. The widely used EC2 instance can be a virtual machine or a dedicated bare metal server. And from serverless lambda computing to parallel computing service the range of compute offering is quite varied to suite diffferent kinds of computing needs. ROSA is a K8s platform from Redhat for microservice deployments. Along with managed Relational Database Systems (RDS) there are Timestream database, graph database Neptune, and DynamoDB NoSQL database. There are in-memory cache called ElastiCache and MongoDB-compatible DocumentDB. Thus there are a large variety of database services to try.

Database offerings from AWS: Amazon DocumentDB is a fully-managed MongoDB-compatible database service. DynamoDB is a managed NoSQL Database. ElastiCache is an in-memory Cache. Amazon Keyspaces is a serverless cassandra-compatible database. Amazon MemoryDB is a fully managed Redis OSS-compatible in-memory database service. Neptune is a fast, reliable graph database built for the cloud.

Amazon Timestream is a fast, scalable, and serverless time series database for IoT and operational applications. RDS is a major Database Service for Managed Relational Databases. RDS offers Blue/Green Deployment model to minimize downtime during upgrades. A Blue/Green Deployment provides a staging system for changes to production databases. There are many RDS Engine options like Aurora (MySQL Compatible), Aurora (PostgreSQL Compatible), MySQL, MariaDB, PostgreSQL, Oracle, Microsoft SQL Server and IBM Db2. Oracle RDS also comes in multitenant architecture which is a container database (CDB) including one or more tenant databases (PDBs). Oracle RDS instance configuration can be Standard classes (includes m classes), Memory optimized classes (includes r and x classes) and Burstable classes (includes t classes). Oracle RDS offers storage autoscaling, provisioned IOPS SSD (io2 etc.) storage volumes. Oracle RDS can be deployed in a HA mode as a Multi-AZ deployment which creates a standby in a different Availability Zone (AZ) to provide data redundancy, eliminate I/O freezes, and minimize latency spikes during system backups. Deployed in a VPC it is a robust AWS offering for handling critical data.

AWS compute service offering is truely rich. The widely used EC2 instance can be a virtual machine or a dedicated baremetal server. And from serverless lambda computing to parallel computing service, the range of compute offering is quite varied to suite diffferent kinds of computing needs.

One can get started with some sample examples.

1-Create an Account.

2-Login to AWS Console using root user's email.

3-Create an EC2 instance and dowload the keypair.

4-Assign a static IP to the EC2 instance.

5-Login using putty from your desktop or laptop.

6-Create a directory called mydirectory1 under ec2-user's home directory.

7-Create a bucket called myawstestbucket1 using s3 service.

8-Upload a sample file from laptop or desktop to that bucket.

9-Configure API access from EC2 to S3.

10-Transfer the file from that bucket to EC2 instance into the directory mydirectory1.

An example backup script that copies from EBS of an EC2 instance to S3.

```
[root@mail backup]# cat backup.sh
cd ~/backup
```

tar  -cvf  temp-backup.tar   /home/bibhuti/Desktop2/apache/apache-tomcat-8.0.33/webapps/template*
aws s3 cp temp-backup.tar s3://ashabackup/khordha1/
[root@mail backup]#
  [root@mail backup]# aws configure
AWS Access Key ID [***************MMGO]:
AWS Secret Access Key [***************ATCP]:
Default region name [us-east-2]:
Default output format [None]:
[root@mail backup]#

IAM: Root is the parent organizational unit (ou) for all child organizational units and accounts in an organization. An organization unit is a group of accounts. If a policy is applied to the root, then it applies to all underlying org units and accounts in the organization. The organization's management account pays bills for all accounts under the organization. Policy is used to manage different features of accounts in an organization. Multi factor authentication or MFA is an additional saftey for accounts. One can login using root account or IAM accounts. Root user has unrestricted privilege and should be very carefully used. Users should login using IAM user using IAM role assigned by the Administrator.

Migration Services: Migration Hub strategy recommendations is very helpful during migration. It helps plan migration and modernization initiatives by suggesting a migration and modernization strategy recommendations as a viable transformation path for applications.

AWS S3: AWS Storage services provides AWS Backup which centrally manages and automates backups across AWS services. EFS is a managed file storage service from AWS. AWS Elastic DR is a scalable cost-effective application recovery to AWS. FSx is a managed third party file system optimized for variety of workloads. S3 is scalable storage in the cloud. S3 glacier is an archive storage. Storage Gateway is a hybrid storage intengration service. AWS buckets are by default with public access prohibited. S3 buckets can be versioned too. By default SSE is used to encrypt the buckets. Bucket life cycle rule is a good feature for moving the objects among different storage tiers thus optimizing cost and retrieval needs.

**Lifecycle rule actions**                    Source: AWS S3 bucket

☑ Transition current versions of objects between storage classes

☑ Transition noncurrent versions of objects between storage classes

☑ Expire current versions of objects

☑ Permanently delete noncurrent versions of objects

☑ Delete expired object delete markers or incomplete multipart uploads

These actions are not supported when filtering by object tags or object size.

## Transition current versions of objects between storage classes

Choose transitions to move current versions of objects between storage classes based on your use requirements. These transitions start from when the objects are created and are consecutively appl

**Choose storage class transitions**                **Days after object creation**

| Standard-IA ▼ | *Number of days* |

A valid integer value is required.

VMware Cloud on AWS: VMware is the leading private cloud provider while AWS is the leading public cloud provider. Both have partnered for many solutions like Data centre extension, cost effective DR solution, Cloud migration and data centre exit, and next generation apps.

IoT services: IoT core connects devices to the cloud. IoT analytics collect, preprocess, store, analyze and visualize data of IoT devices. IoT greengrass deploy and run code on devices. IoT SiteWise helps in data driven decisions in industrial operations. IoT Events detect and respond to events from IoT sensors and industrial IoT equipment. IoT makes the devices intelligent and the streaming data can enter into data pipelines and arrive in Redshift DWH for analytics.

AWS Data Pipeline: It moves, integrates and processes data across compute and strorage in both AWS and On-prem. It supports integration of data and activites across AWS regions. In AWS Data Pipeline, a data node defines the location and type of data that a pipeline activity uses as input or output. AWS Data Pipeline supports different types of data nodes like

DynamoDBDataNode, SqlDataNode, RedshiftDataNode, and S3DataNode. An activity is a pipeline component defining the work to perform. AWS Data Pipeline provides several activities for common scenarios, such as moving data from one location to another, running Hive queries, and so on. AWS Data Pipeline supports activities like CopyActivity, EmrActivity, HiveActivity (a hive query on EMR), HiveCopyActivity, PigActivity, RedshiftCopyActivity, ShellCommandActivity, and SqlActivity.

Some Migration & Transfer Services in AWS:

Application Discovery Service discovers on-prem application inventory and dependencies.

AWS Application Migration Service (MGN) automates lift-and-shift migration.

Database Migration Service is a Managed Database Migration Service.I t is a major service.

DataSync simplifies, automates, and accelerates moving of data.

AWS Mainframe Modernization modernizes Mainframe workloads.

AWS Migration Hub simplifies and accelerates the migration of data centers to AWS.

AWS Snow Family is used for large scale data transport.

AWS Transfer Family provides fully managed support for SFTP, FTPS, FTP, and AS2.

AWS App2Container: It is a CLI tool for modernizing .NET, and Java applications into containerized applications.

For Data Collection during Migration, AWS offers an ova file AWSMHubApplicationDataCollector.ova

A data collector uses a S3 bucket and an IAM role to transfer the data collected to DMS.

AWS DMS support for AWS CloudFormation: One can provision AWS DMS resources using AWS CloudFormation. CloudFormation is used for automation of infrastructure management or deployment.

Oracle LogMiner or DMS Binary Reader for CDC: In AWS DMS, these two methods are used for reading redo logs when doing change data capture with Oracle as a source. LogMiner is an Oracle API to read online redo logs and archived redo log files. Binary Reader is a DMS method to read and parse the raw redo log files directly.

What are the sources for DMS?

An Oracle database as a source for AWS DMS.

A Microsoft SQL Server database as a source for AWS DMS.

Microsoft Azure SQL database as a source for AWS DMS.

Microsoft Azure SQL Managed Instance as a source for AWS DMS.

Google Cloud for MySQL as a source for AWS DMS.

A PostgreSQL database as an AWS DMS source.

A MySQL-compatible database as a source for AWS DMS.

An SAP ASE database as a source for AWS DMS.

MongoDB as a source for AWS DMS.

Amazon DocumentDB (with MongoDB compatibility) as a source for AWS DMS.

Amazon S3 as a source for AWS DMS.

IBM Db2 for Linux, Unix, and Windows database (Db2 LUW) as a source for AWS DMS.

IBM Db2 for z/OS databases as a source for AWS DMS.

If migration is heterogeneous (between two databases of different engine types), one can use the AWS Schema Conversion Tool (AWS SCT) to generate a complete target schema. Any dependencies between tables such as FK constraints need to be disabled during migration's "full load" and "cached change apply" phases. When performance is an issue, removing or disabling of secondary indexes during the migration process helps.

AWS Database Migration Service (AWS DMS)  migrates relational databases,  data warehouses, NoSQL  databases, and other types of data  stores. It can migrate data into the AWS cloud or between combinations of cloud and on-prem setups.

With DMS, one can perform one-time migrations, and then replicate ongoing changes to   keep sources and targets in sync. If one wants to migrate to a different database engine, one can use the AWS Schema Conversion Tool  to translate database schema to the new platform. And then AWS DMS can migrate the data.

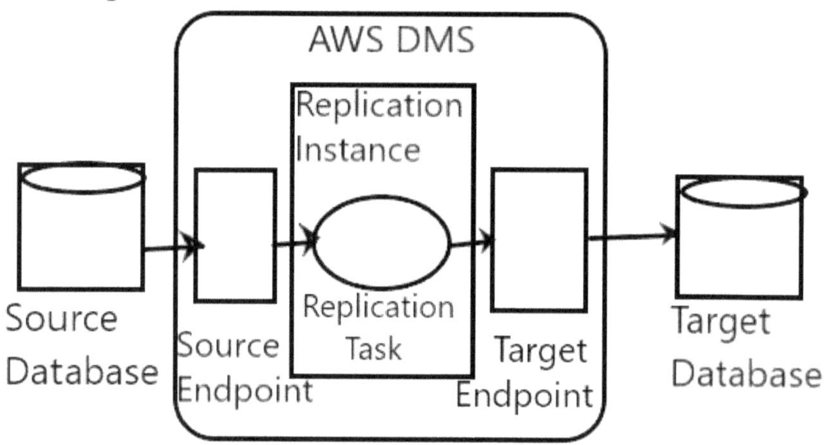


EC2: The aspects of EC2 to explore are:
Instances
Instance Types
Launch Templates
Spot Requests
Savings Plans

Reserved Instances
Dedicated Hosts
Capacity Reservations

Compute Images:

AMIs: EC2 Image Builder is a fully-managed service that makes it easy to build, customize and deploy OS images without writing scripts. Image type can be a Docker image or Amazon Machine Image. Amazon Machine Image Builder supports Amazon Linux, Windows, Ubuntu, CentOS, RHEL, and SLES. Storage options can be set like volume iops, ebs volume size, encryption, snapshot. Enhanced scanning can also be enabled during image building.

For docker image buiding, image can be based on ECR image(Image hosted in ECR repository) or Docker Hub image(Public image hosted in Docker Hub repository). Docker Image Operating System (OS) supported by image builder are Amazon Linux, Windows, Ubuntu, and CentOS.

Services for Management & Governance:

AWS Auto Scaling: It enables to quickly scale entire application on AWS.

AWS Chatbot: It is ChatOps service for AWS.

CloudFormation: It creates and manages Resources with Templates.

CloudTrail: It tracks User Activity and API Usage.

CloudWatch: It monitors Resources and Applications.

AWS Compute Optimizer: It recommends optimal AWS Compute resources for workloads.

AWS Config: It tracks Resource Inventory and Changes.

Control Tower: It is the easiest way to set up and govern a secure, compliant multi-account environment.

Amazon Grafana: It is a fully managed Grafana service for interactive data visualizations and dashboarding.

AWS Health Dashboard: It is a personalized view of AWS service health.

Incident Manager: It is an automated incident response plans in AWS Systems Manager.

Launch Wizard: It is a guided deployment for Enterprise applications and complex workloads.

AWS License Manager: It sets rules to manage, discover, and report third-party license usage proactively.

OpsWorks: It is for configuration management with Chef and Puppet

AWS Organizations: It is used for central governance and management across AWS accounts.

Amazon Prometheus: It is a fully managed Prometheus-compatible monitoring service.

AWS Proton: It manages infrastructure.

AWS Resilience Hub: It provides a central place to define, validate, and track resiliency of applications.

Container Services:

Elastic Container Registry: It is a fully-managed Docker container registry to share and deploy container software, publicly or privately.

Elastic Container Service: It is a highly secure, reliable, and scalable way to run containers.

Elastic Kubernetes Service: It is a trusted way to start, run, and scale Kubernetes.

ROSA: It is a fully managed Red Hat OpenShift service on AWS.

Machine Learning Tools and Services from AWS:

Amazon Augmented AI: It implements human review of machine learning predictions.

Amazon Bedrock: It is used to build and scale generative AI applications with foundation models (FMs).

Amazon CodeGuru: It is an intelligent recommendations for building and running modern applications.

Amazon Comprehend: It analyzes unstructured Text.

Amazon Comprehend Medical: It uses ML to extract insights and relationships from medical text.

AWS DeepComposer: It allows developers to get started with Generative AI.

AWS DeepRacer: It is a fully autonomous 1/18th scale race car, driven by machine learning.

Amazon DevOps Guru: It is a ML-powered cloud operations service to improve application availability.

Amazon Forecast: It is a fully-managed service for accurate time-series forecasting.

Amazon Fraud Detector: It detects online fraud faster using machine learning.

AWS HealthImaging: It stores, analyzes, and shares medical images.

AWS HealthLake: It makes sense of health data.

AWS HealthOmics: It transform omics data into insights.

Amazon Kendra: It is a highly accurate enterprise search service powered by machine learning.

Amazon Lex: It builds Voice and Text Chatbots.

Amazon Lookout for Equipment: It detects abnormal equipment behavior by analyzing sensor data.

Amazon Lookout for Metrics: It detects anomalies in business metrics and quickly understands reason.

Amazon Lookout for Vision: It identifies defects using computer vision to autate quality inspection.

Amazon Monitron: It is an end-to-end system for equipment monitoring.

AWS Panorama: It enables computer vision applications at the edge.

Amazon Polly: It turns Text into Lifelike Speech.

Amazon Q: It is a generative-AI powered assistant from AWS.

Amazon Q Business: It is a generative AI-powered enterprise assistant.

Amazon Rekognition: It searches and analyzes Images.

Amazon SageMaker: It builds, trains, and deploys Machine Learning Models.

Amazon Textract: It easily extracts text and data from virtually any document.

Amazon Transcribe: It is a powerful Speech Recognition tool.

Amazon Translate: It is used for powerful Neural Machine Translation.

VPC:

VPC Peering: A VPC peering connection is a connection between two VPCs enabling routing of traffic between them privately. The two VPCs can be from two different accounts in two different regions too.

A subnet in a VPC can be in any AZ(Availability Zone) of the VPC. It must be from the CIDR block of the VPC. Every VPC has a main route route table. By default, there is a route in main RT to IGW (internet GW) which allows outbound traffic to internet. The target "local" in main RT allows inteconnection by default among the IPs of the VPC's CIDR block. An egress only internet gateway in a VPC allows only outbound connection to internet and blocks connections initiated from internet.

DHCP option set on VPC provides a standard for passing configuration information to hosts on a TCP/IP network. Informations like Domain name servers, NTP servers, and NetBIOS name servers are set with DHCP option set on VPC. NAT GW is a highly available, managed Network Address Translation (NAT) service that instances in private subnets use to connect to services in other VPCs, on-premises networks, or the internet. NAT Gateway forwards traffic from private subnets to other networks. NAT GW can be either public or private.

AWS Network Firewall: It is a managed network firewall service for VPC. It is a stateful, managed network firewall and intrusion prevention/detection service which allows customers to filter traffic at the perimeter of VPC. It inspects and manages network traffic between VPC and Internet Gateway, NAT Gateway, or VPN gateway. This Firewall also provides detailed logs and alerts on how it handles the packets that it inspects. A TLS inspection configuration is used by Network Firewall to decrypt and re-encrypt firewall's inbound and outbound traffic encrypted by Secure Socket Layer (SSL)/Transport Layer Security (TLS). It uses a Certificate. Network Firewall Resource groups allow to tag and group AWS resources like EC2 instances, to manage in a single group that one can reference in a stateful rule group.

AWS Storage Gateway offers file-based (S3 File Gateway and FSx File Gateway), volume-based (Volume Gateway), and tape-based (Tape Gateway) storage solutions. Using a volume gateway in cached volumes mode by using cached volumes, customer can use Amazon S3 as primary data storage, while retaining frequently accessed data locally in Storage Gateway. A Volume GW in Cached Volume mode is shown here. After installing the Storage Gateway software appliance (the VM on a host in On-prem data center), AWS Management Console is used to provision storage volumes backed by Amazon S3. One can also provision storage volumes programmatically using Storage Gateway API, or the AWS SDK libraries. The storage volumes then can be mounted to on-prem application servers as iSCSI devices.

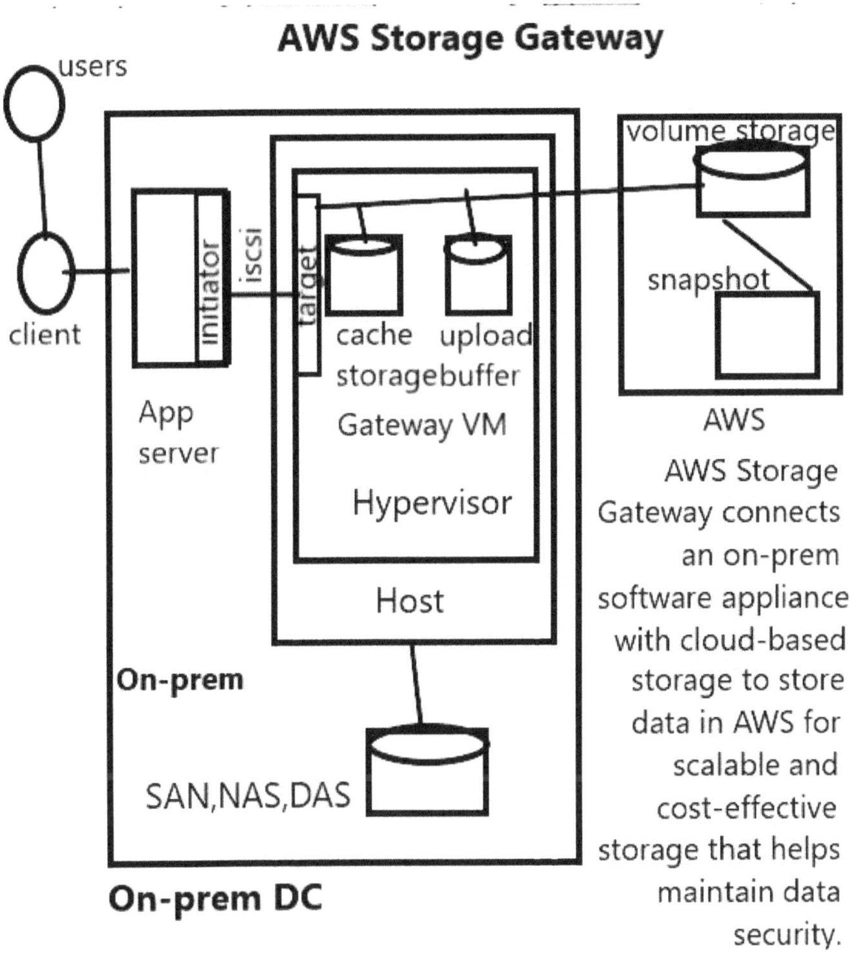



Incremental backups, or snapshots, of storage volumes can be taken in Amazon S3. These PIT snapshots are stored as EBS snapshots. One can restore EBS snapshot to a gateway storage volume to recover from a backup of data. Alternatively, for snapshots less than 16 TiB, one can directly use the snapshot as a new EBS volume. This new EBS volume can be attached to an Amazon EC2 instance. All gateway data and snapshot data for cached volumes stored in S3 are encrypted at rest using server-side encryption. But, one can't access this data with S3 API or Management Console.

For backup and recovery which requires massive storage, these On-prem-AWS solutions can be explored for a cost effective and efficient alternative.

CHAPTER THREE

# IBM Cloud

A high level network architecture is given here for beginners.

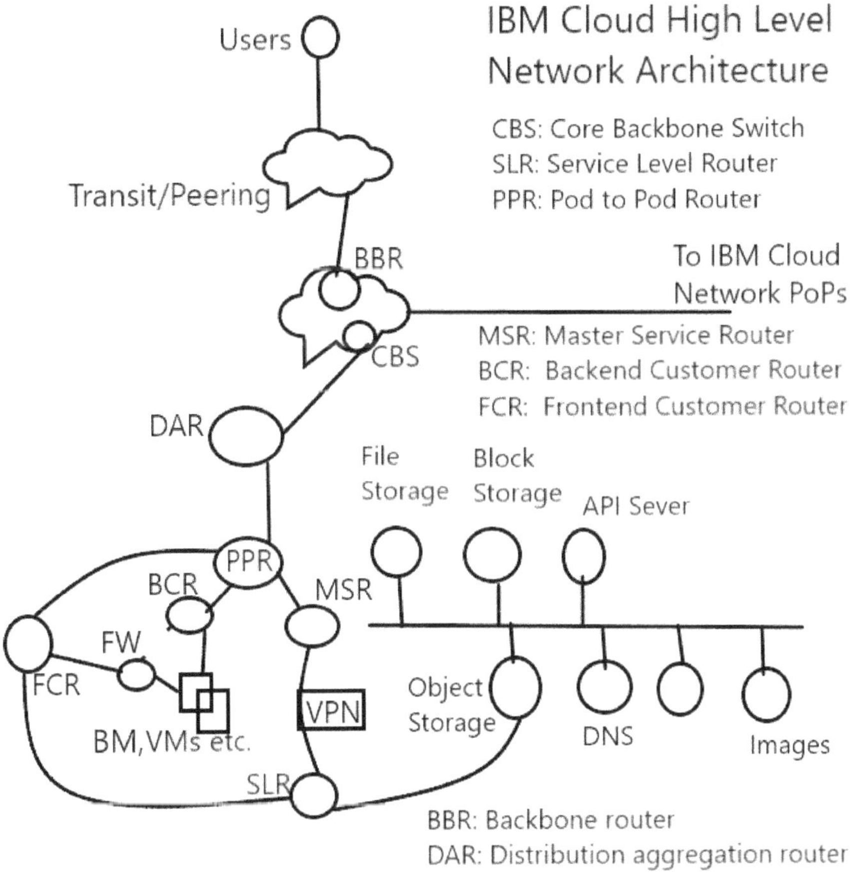

A sample use of local and global Transit Gateways used in conjuction with DL(Direct Link) given here to compose connectivity aspects of accounts spread across VPCs and Classic Infrastructure.

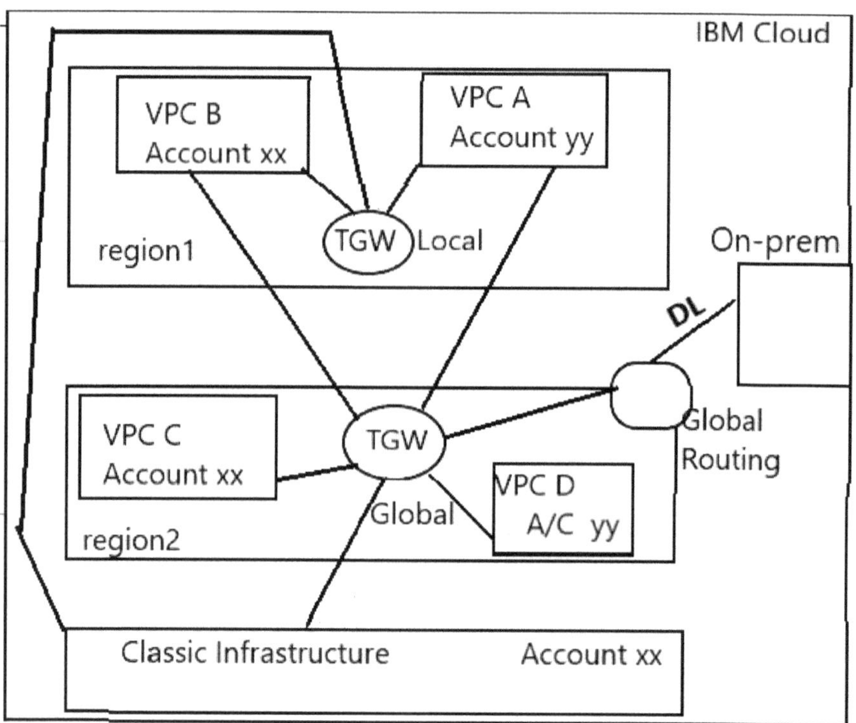

What are the different categories of services? What Products and services can be used from IBM or its Partners on IBM Cloud?

IBM Cloud provides both VPC and Classic Infrastructure based services. In storage, there are Block Storage, File Storage, Object Storage, and Cloud Backup. In Network, IBM Cloud offers CDN, DNS, IP Management, Global IPs, Load Balancing, VPN Gateways, Transit Gateways, Direct Link etc. IBM Cloud provides K8S, VMware Clouds, DevOps and Satellite Services. It also provides several data migration services. On-prem IBM Power Servers can be migrated to Power VSI using PowerVS Migration as a Service. VMware solutions on IBM Cloud can be used for Baremetal services where dedicated infrastructure is required. IBM Cloud also provides several engineered product deployment like SAP, SAP HANA, Oracle on PowerVS platforms. These PowerVS workspaces can be connnected to other cloud services using Tansit Gateways. One can use one's own AIX, IBM i, and Linux images on PowerVS services in cloud. In Backup and Recovery area, there are several VTL services either from IBM or from its partners. FalconStor StorSafe VTL for Power On-Premises can be used to decrease on-premise backup storage capacity while improving backup solutions using cloud. HDM VMware Workload Analyzer from PrimaryIO is an workload analyzer transparently monitoring current VMware virtual platform IO to plan for migration. IBM has partnerships with many different Technology Expert Labs worldwide to jointly work on cloud migration and BAU (business as usual) solutions on cloud.

How are the services delivered or provisioned? Services can be delivered using Cloud Paks, Helm Charts, OVA Images, Operators, Server Images and Terraform.

What are the different deployment target for the services? Diffrent targets where services can be deployed are IBM Cloud Kubernetis Service, Power Systems Virtual Server, Red Hat Openshift, VMware vCenter Server, Virtual private cloud(x86), and IBM Cloud Schematics etc. Thus each deployment target requires some specific delivery modes, and skilled cloud professionals can definitely help in a big way both during migration and post migration periods. In addition to traditional skills like Virtualization, Docker, OS, Database, Web Server, Application Server, Inetegration, Analytics, ML, AI, Hardware, WAN, LAN, SAN, NAS, DR, HA and Monitoring etc. a successful career in cloud requires to understand Cloud Migration Sevices, Cloud IAM, Cloud Provisioning and Monitor/Manage of different services in hybrid and multi cloud environments.

Accounts and Billing: Different cloud tools and services are billed either monthly or hourly. Below is an example billing sheet for a Baremetal server from IBM Cloud provisioned using VMware cloud foundation service from VMware.

# Detailed Billing

Cost/Month: xxxx$

Baremetal host : xyz.sl.ibm.com

| | Category Group |
|---|---|
| Server: Quad Intel Xeon Platinum 8260 (96 Cores, 2.4 GHz) | Server |
| RAM: 768 GB RAM | RAM |
| Second Processor: Intel Xeon Platinum 8260 (96 Cores, 2.4 GHz)* | Second Processor |
| Public Bandwidth: 20000 GB Bandwidth Allotment | Public Bandwidth |
| Primary IP Addresses: 1 IP Address (169.47.216.128/27) | Primary IP Addresses |
| Third Hard Drive: 960GB SSD (3 DWPD) | Third Hard Drive |
| Third Processor: Intel Xeon Platinum 8260 (96 Cores, 2.4 GHz)* | Third Processor |
| Second Hard Drive: 960GB SSD (3 DWPD) | Second Hard Drive |
| Fourth Processor: Intel Xeon Platinum 8260 (96 Cores, 2.4 GHz)* | Fourth Processor |
| Public Network Port: 10 Gbps Redundant Public Uplinks* | Public Network Port |
| Disk Controller: RAID | Disk Controller |
| Power Supply: Redundant Power Supply | Power Supply |
| Fourth Hard Drive: 960GB SSD (3 DWPD) | Fourth Hard Drive |
| Operating System: VMware Cloud Foundation with VMware | Operating System |
| First Hard Drive: 960GB SSD (3 DWPD) | First Hard Drive |
| Uplink Port Speeds: 10 Gbps Redundant Public & Private Network | Uplink Port Speeds |

# CHAPTER FOUR

# AZURE

IAM (Identity and Access Management) is the component of Azure Cloud used for managing access and authorization. A brief overview of a flow of a resource request can be useful. Using WS-Fed (Web Services Federation) for eaxample, Identity & Authorization can be handled by customer's own IAM Services. A customer may choose to handle IAM using its own set of Active Directory Servers. Thus, Azure IAM handshakes with IAM framework of customer. This way transition to cloud for customer with a huge employee or partner base and many on-prem applications is smooth. Security is an important factor in deciding adoption of cloud.

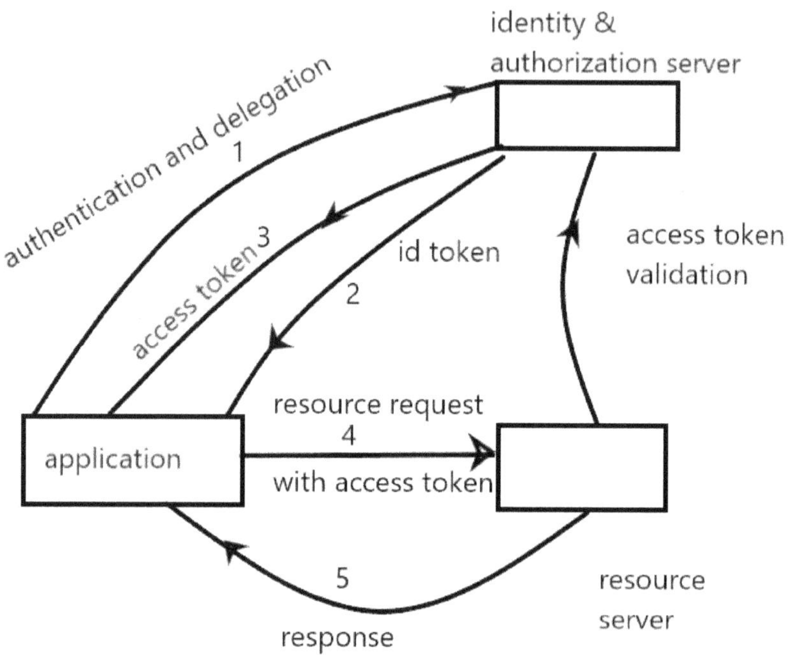

Different authentication and authorization methods can be used for IAM. Thus, a customer can either use any one standard or a combination of standards suiting their application needs. For example, one application say, AAP (Ansible Automation Platform) from Redhat may handle user authentication using SAML, while another application can choose OIDC. One Application can call another application with Tokens as well. Which protocol to use and in which situation is a separate topic addressed by coroprate security architecture and standards, and a cloud provider should be flexible to inegrate with different standards.

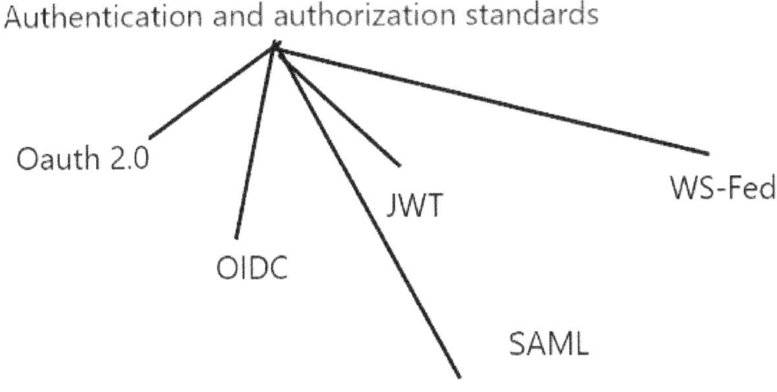


How are the resources organized in terms of ownership? The resources in Azure can be VMs, Clusters, Caches, Databases, Virtual Networks, IPs, Load balancers, Object Storages and Disks etc. Resources are grouped into Resource Groups which in turn are managed under subscriptions. For example, different BU (business units) can go for different subscriptions. Level of access to subscriptions may vary. A tenant may have access to one or more subscriptions at various levels like reader, contributor, owner etc. AAD (Azure Active Directory) can integrate with customer's own AD systems as well.

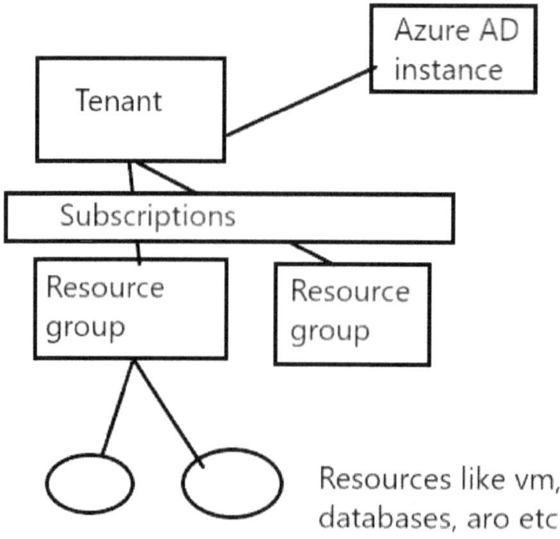

Vnet or virtual network is a networking resource analogus to VPC. It contains several resources like service end points, service links, databases, clusters, caches, vms, applications etc. It is divided into subnets. A Vnet can be spread across some AZ or availabiliy zones. ARO is a K8s offering (explained in K8s chapter) used for composing cloud native or microservices. ARO or Azure redhat openshift from Redhat is a managed service that can be explored as a container platform for modernization and transformation of infrastrructure and applications. Another very critical and useful product in SD networking is Virtual WAN. Another useful service is Azure Arc for resource management and governance. Using Arc resources spread across cloud and on-prem can be managed.

Azure Redis Cache: It comes with different configurations. One example Redis Cluster can be a Zone-redundant Premium 26 GB (2 x 13 GB) with

AOF as Data Persistence. Utility redis-cli can be used to login to the redis cluster used for PoC.

Example: redis-cli -p 6379 -a <accesskey> -h pochost.redis.cache.windows.net

At a broad level a Redis Cache Architecture from Azure is given below considering how frequently transactions are persisted, where the export goes, where replication happens and what the default PITR (point in time recovery) is. During PoC, along with cost estimation all other aspects like total memory capacity of redis cluster, data persistence using AOF or RDB, Storage Account configuration, read/write latency time, and Cache Performance metrics etc. should be carefully evaluated. Memory caching is nowadays an important part of application architecture for fast response time.

AOF can have a higher performance impact than RDB, when using the always fsync policy, as it logs every write operation and syncs file more frequently. RDB has a lower performance impact, as it takes snapshots of in-memory data and saves to disk periodically. Still, these design decisions should be handled by architects and deveopers. Storage Account can be Zonal or Global etc. influencing HA and DR policy of customers. Backup frequency also matters. Other configurations like SSL/Non-SSL, number of Availability Zones in AZ configuration etc. should also be evaluated.

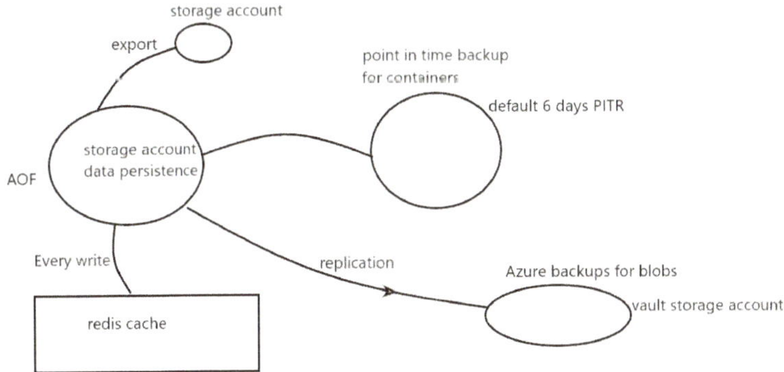

A 2 shard Redis Cluster deployed in a Vnet(Virtual Network) and accessed from an application running on an ARO (Azure Redhat Openshift) Cluster deployed into same Vnet. It is HA capable as it is deployed or installed across two Availability Zones(AZ). Each shard has a primary and a replica. Primary accepts R/W requests. Primary and Replica are automatically synchonized.

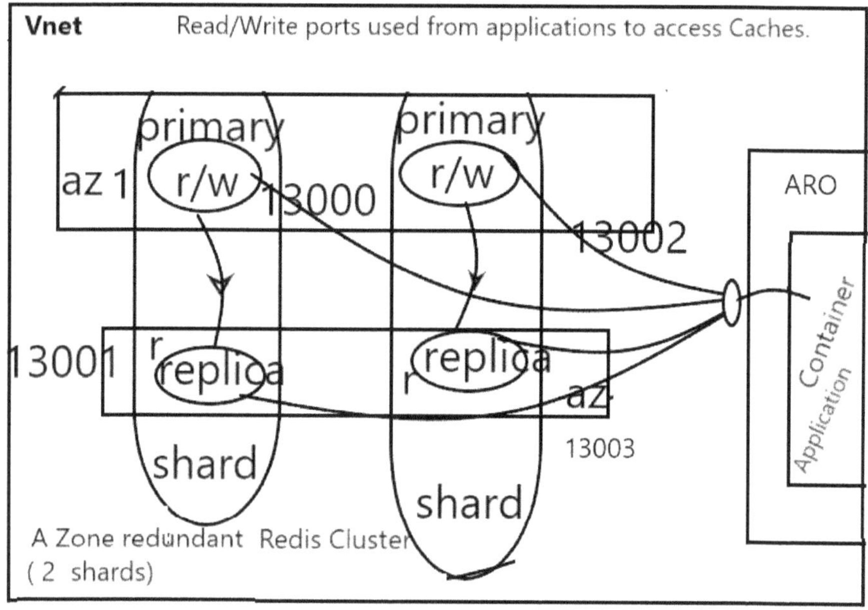

Benchmarks: There are many native tools available for storage, database, & in-memory cache bench markings. redis-benchmark is a utility available to evaluate a redis cluster's performance.

Examples: redis-benchmark --cluster -p 10000 -a <Access-Key> -h pochost.westus3.redisenterprise.cache.azure.net -t set -r 100000 -n 1000000

====== SET ======
1000000 requests completed in 13.53 seconds
50 parallel clients
3 bytes payload

keep alive: 1

cluster mode: yes (8 masters)

multi-thread: yes

threads: 8

Latency by percentile distribution:

0.000% <= 0.184 milliseconds.

50.000% <= 0.528 milliseconds.

75.000% <= 0.707 milliseconds.

...

100.000% <= 1026.535 milliseconds.

Summary:

Throughput summary: 69842.08 requests per second.

latency summary (msec):

avg min p50 p95 p99 max

0.680 0.176 0.527 1.007 4.271 1025.535

For example, pgbench utility can be used for postgres database bench marking with multiple rounds of tests with different number of concurrent jobs.

psql

create database standard_benchmark;

pgbench --initialize --scale=10 standard_benchmark

Test-1 pgbench --time=300 -c 10 standard_benchmark

Test-2 pgbench --time=300 -c 10 -M extended standard_benchmark

Test-3 pgbench --time=300 -c 10 --vacuum-all --jobs 10 standard_benchmark

Test-4 pgbench --time=300 -c 10 --vacuum-all --jobs 10 -M extended standard_benchmark

Test-5 pgbench --time=600 -c 50 --vacuum-all --jobs 50 standard_benchmark

Test-6 pgbench --time=600 -c 50 --vacuum-all --jobs 50 -M extended standard_benchmark

Test-7 pgbench --time=3600 -c 100 --vacuum-all --jobs 100 standard_benchmark

Test-8 pgbench --time=3600 -c 100 --vacuum-all --jobs 100 -M extended standard_benchmark

One example:

```
sh-4.4$ pgbench --time=300 -c 10 standard_benchmark

starting vacuum...end.
transaction type: <builtin: TPC-B (sort of)>
scaling factor: 10
query mode: simple
number of clients: 10
number of threads: 1
duration: 300 s
number of transactions actually processed: 210124

latency average = 14.280 ms
tps = 700.265859 (including connections establishing)
tps = 700.275067 (excluding connections establishing)
```

***

Kubestr: It is another useful tool for Container. It is a collection of tools to discover, validate and evaluate K8s storage options. With growing adoption of K8s, persistent storage offerings too grow. The CSI (Container Storage Interface) has enabled storage providers to develop drivers rapidly. There are many different CSI drivers available today. Along with the existing in-tree providers, these high number of options make right container storage selection difficult. Kubestr assists in identifing various storage options present in a K8s cluster. It also validate if storage options are configured correctly or not. Example: Evaluate a storage class using benchmarking tool FIO.

```
./kubestr fio -s <storage class>
```

***

Azure Virtual WAN: It is a networking service which brings many networking, security, and routing functionalities together providing a single interface. Azure regions serve as hubs which one can choose to connect to. All hubs are connected in full mesh in a Standard Virtual WAN. This makes it easy for the user to use the Microsoft backbone for any-to-any (any spoke) connectivity. A virtual hub is a virtual network with gateways for site-to-site, ExpressRoute, or point-to-site. A virtual hub gateway isn't a virtual network gateway. A site-to-site connection traffic goes through the virtual hub gateway. Thus, a VNet don't need its own virtual network gateway.

Some features of Azure Virtual WAN:

Branch connectivity.

Site-to-site VPN connectivity.

Remote user VPN connectivity (point-to-site).

Private connectivity (ExpressRoute).

Intra-cloud connectivity (transitive connectivity for virtual networks).

VPN ExpressRoute inter-connectivity.

Routing, Azure Firewall, and encryption for private connectivity.

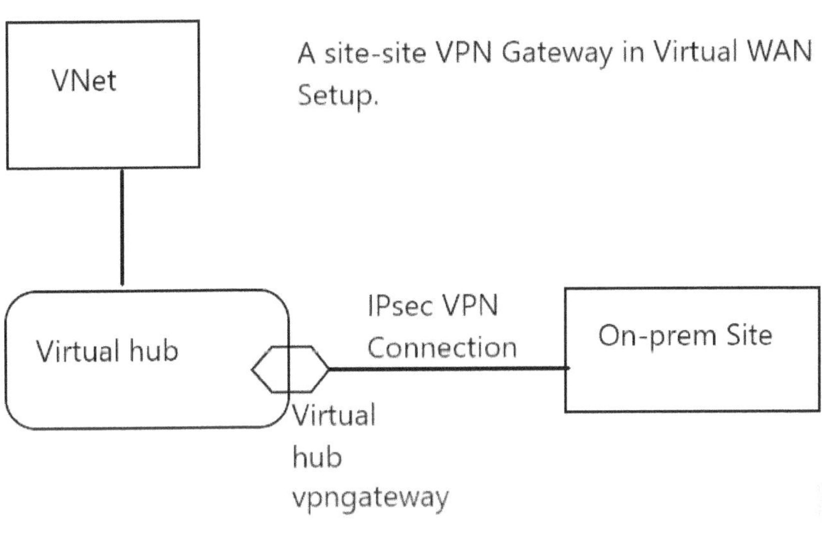

# CHAPTER FIVE

# GOOGLE CLOUD

Google Cloud offers a rich set of tools and services.
Some DBaaS products are useful for modernization of workloads.

DBaaS products from Google Cloud

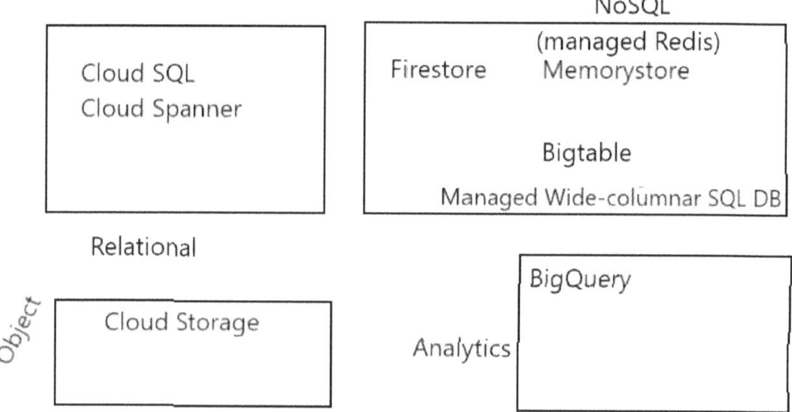


What is a Google Data Lake?

Data Lake is a secure and scalable data platform allowing enterprises to load, store, process, and analyze any type or volume of data. Data ingestion can be batch or stream. IoT devices and sensors provide streaming data. For analysis and visualization of data several tools like DWH, NoSQL, Dashboards, ML/AI and Notebooks are used. Data lake is a secured and managed solution providing BI(business intelligence), Data Science(Vertex

AI), Data engineering, and Data integration services. Data lake is a Data Platform for various business needs of an organization. While on-prem data lakes are migrated to cloud they can be transformed and modernized as well to exploit various cloud native and opensource integration services making Data Lake a highly desirable business solution.

How is the Google Data Lake filled?
Filling of Data Lake depends on the type of data. For on-prem with good network online transfers can be used. For region to region transfer possibly involving multi cloud cloud storage transfer services can be used. In case on-prem network is bad and data is huge, transfer appliance should be used. For getting data from DWH, market & SaaS databases Bigquery transfer service can be tested.

How can google assist in digital transformation journey?
There are different Google cloud services to assist in digital transformation journey which is a prime driver for cloud adoption. For movement of data there are various database and compute services Cloud SQL, Cloud Spanner, and Bare metal servers. Once data is migrated for application migrations there are compute engine and networking services. For optimization for the cloud there are K8s, App Engine, Cloud Run etc. And for on-going transformation of business there are Data Lake, ML and Bigquery platforms.

What are the various ETL and ELT tool offered by Google Cloud?

For data ingestion at any scale there are pub/sub, data transfer services and IOT Core. For data transformation and streaming pipelines there are Dataflow, Dataproc, Dataprep by Trifecta and Cloud Data Fusion services. For Data warehousing and Data Lake solutions google offers Bigquery and Cloud Storage. And for Advanced analytics google services to explore are Vertex AI, Google Data Studio, Notebooks, Looker, BI tools from technology partners and Google Sheets etc.

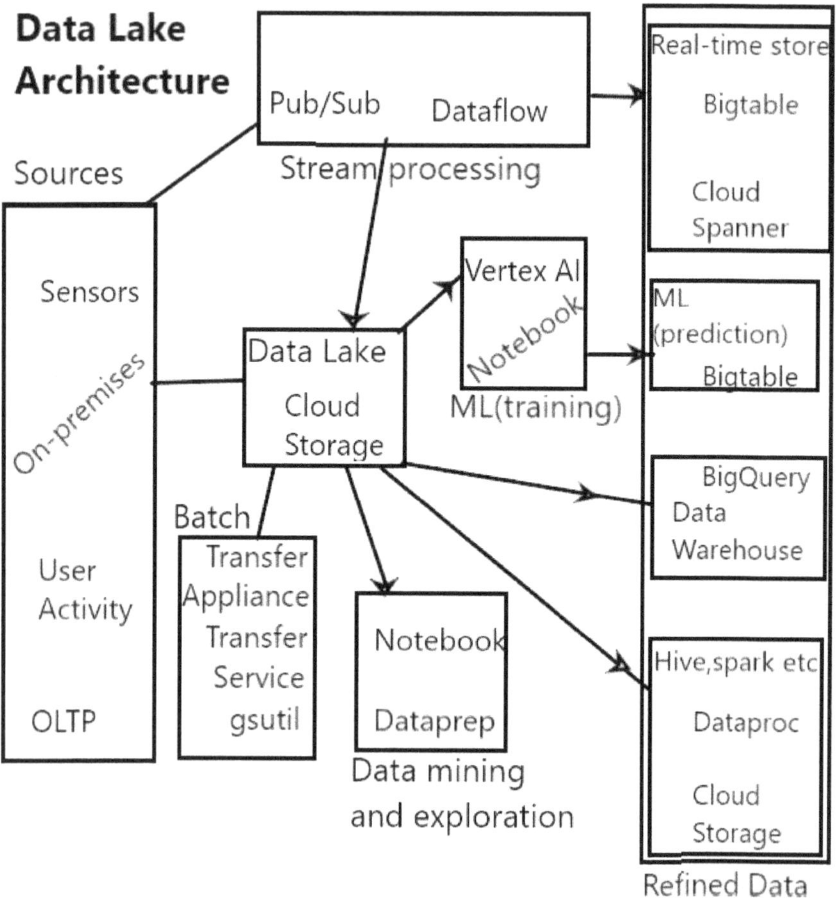


Bigtable NoSQL distributed database: It is good for applications needing high throughput and scalability for key-value data, where each value is typically less than 10 MB. Bigtable storage engine is good for batch MapReduce operations, stream processing and analytics, as well as ML applications.

Each cluster has nodes and each node
is   responsible for some of the shards
or pieces of data.

## HA and regional resilience

## A Bigtable instance with four clusters

With  Multi-cluster routing, Bigtable automatically fails
over to other region if application can't connect one region.

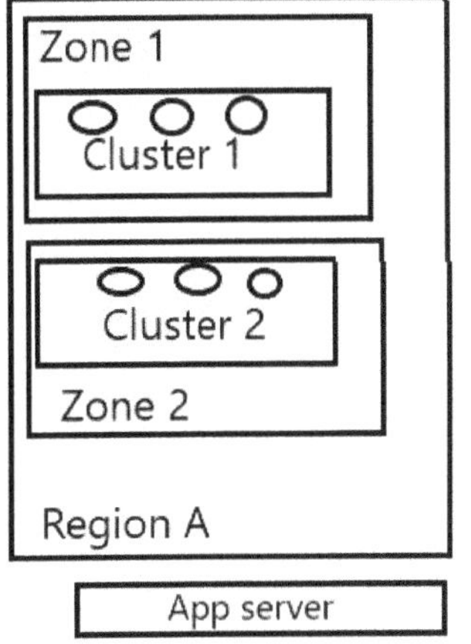


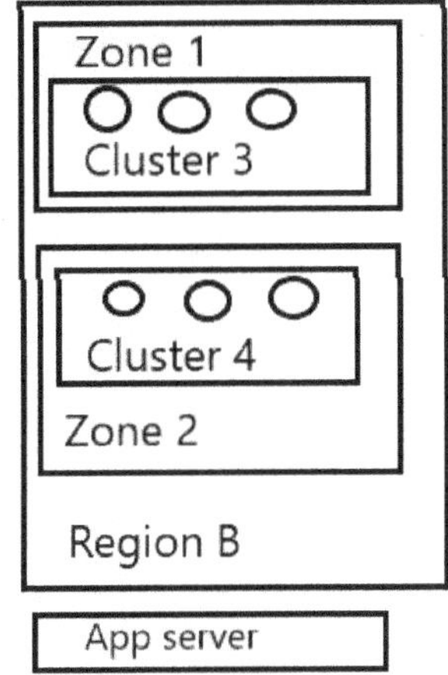


How does a cluster look?

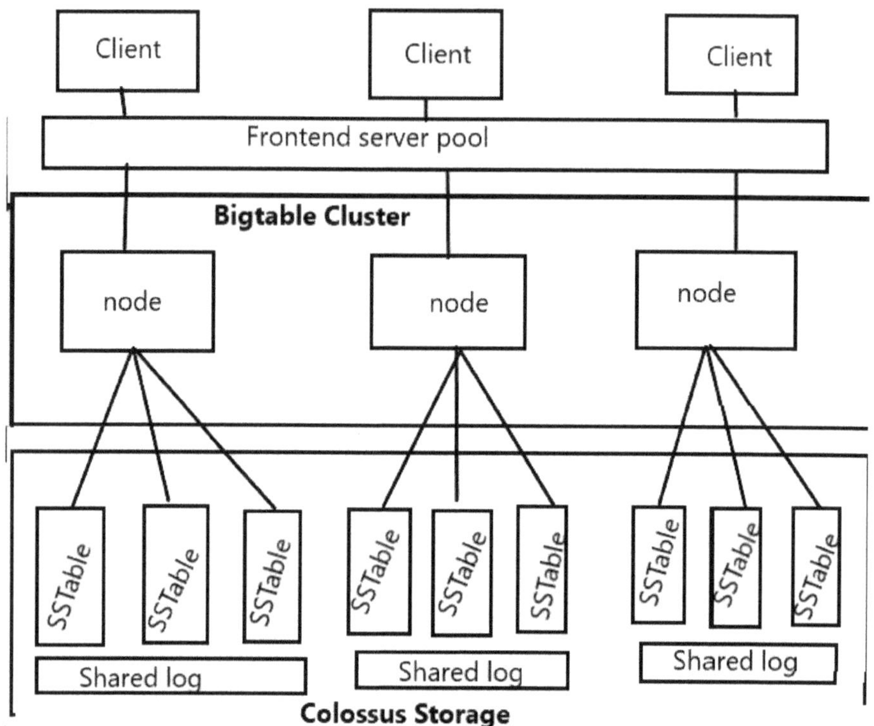

Bigtable can be used to store and query following types of data:

Time-series Data: CPU and memory usage.
Marketing Data: Purchase histories.
Financial Data: Transaction histories, stock prices etc.
IoT Data: Usage reports from energy meters & home appliances.
Graph Data: Information about how users are connected to one another.

Bigtable Storage Model: Bigtable stores data in massively scalable tables. Each table is a sorted key-value map. The table is composed of rows. Each row describes a single entity, and columns containing individual values for each row. Each row is indexed by a single row key. And columns related to one another are grouped into a column family. Each column is identified by a combination of column family and a column qualifier which is a unique name within the column family.

Each intersection of a row and column can have multiple cells. Each cell contains a unique timestamped version of data for that row and column. Storing many cells in a column provides a track of how the stored data for that row and column has changed over time. Bigtable tables are sparse; That is, if a column is not used in a particular row, it does not take up any space.

Shards: One bigtable table is sharded into blocks of contiguous rows, called tablets. It balances the workload of queries. Tablets are stored on Colossus(Google's file system) in SSTable format. A SSTable structure provides a persistent, ordered immutable map from keys to values. Each tablet is associated with a specific Bigtable node. In addition to SSTable files, all writes are also stored in shared log as soon as they are acknowledged by Bigtable.This increases durability.

Data is not stored in Bigtable nodes themselves; Each node has pointers to a set of tablets.This helps in:

Rebalancing tablets from one node is quick as only the pointers for each node are updated.

Recovery from failure of a node is fast, as only metadata is migrated to the replacement node.

When a Bigtable node fails, data is not lost.

Consistency model: Single-cluster Bigtable instances give strong consistency. Multi-cluster instances provide eventual consistency,but for some use cases they can be adjusted to provide read-your-writes consistency or strong consistency, depending on workload, and app profile settings.

Request routing: It happens with app profiles. It controls which clusters handle incoming requests from an application.

Single-cluster routing: It sends all requests to a single cluster.

Multi-cluster routing: It sends requests to the nearest available cluster in an instance, including following options:

Any cluster: Any cluster in the instance can receive requests.

Cluster group routing: Only a specified group of clusters in the instance can receive requests.

Backups: Bigtable backups save a copy of a table's schema and data which can be restored to a new table at a later time. Using backups and backup copies, customer can restore to a new table in any region or project with a Bigtable instance, regardless source table location.

CDC: Bigtable provides change data capture(CDC) as change streams. Change streams can be read by Dataflow to support data analytics, audits, and also triggering downstream application logic if required.

Data compression: Random data cannot be compressed as efficiently as patterned data. Patterned data includes text. Compression works best when identical values are close to each other. If row keys are arranged, so that rows with identical chunks of data are next to each other, the data can be compressed efficiently. Bigtable compresses values up to 1 MiB in size. Values larger than 1 MiB, needs to be compressed first before writing to Bigtable, so CPU cycles, server memory, and network bandwidth can be saved.

Another important Database to explore during migration or modernization is Cloud Spanner RDBMS.

Cloud Spanner suits applications that require:

SQL RDBMS with joins and secondary indexes.

Buil-in HA

Strong global consistency

Database sizes that exceed 2TB

High IOPS

For Migration Google has a useful service called Actifio Go.

Source: https://partner.cloudskillsboost.google/course_template/308

# Inside Track: Install, Deploy and Configure Actifio GO Solutions

Actifio GO for Google Cloud is a SaaS offering which enables powerful enterprise class backup and recovery for Google Cloud resident and on-premises workloads. Actifio now supports backup, disaster recovery and rapid database cloning of Oracle on Bare Metal Solution on Google Cloud besides other enterprise workloads including SAP HANA, SQL Server, and others. This course provides a deep dive into at the preparation and deployment of the Actifio GO solution and its constituent components. Each module contains demos and explanations of each component. The Actifio GO training was originally designed for and only made available to Google Teams, however we've recognized how beneficial it would be for our Partners and are now offering our Partners exclusive access to the Actifio training and products, so they can benefit from the demos and best practices and bring them to their Google Cloud Customers.

Anthos is an useful service to manage services deployed across GKE and On-prem GKE.

Google Networking Products:

Dedicated Interconnect

Partner Interconnect
When on-prem DC can't reach dedicated
interconnect co-location facility.

Direct Peering
Customer Router in same Google PoP

Carrier Peering
Direct access through a Service Provider.

IPSec VPN Protocol

Ways to connect to Google Cloud from on-prem

Google Cloud Load Balancers:

Cloud LB is distributed software-defined managed service. A cloud load balancer can be in front of different traffic:

https
tcp
ssl
udp

It provides single and cross-region load balancing with automatic   multi-region failover.  It can be global as well.

# CHAPTER SIX

# ORACLE CLOUD INFRASTRUCTURE

Oracle is the leading Relational DBMS in the world. Oracle RAC is the only active-active, horizontally and vertically scalable database cluster driving critical applications world wide. Oracle databases are now available in major clouds. Oracle Database@Azure, Oracle Database@Google Cloud and Exadata Cloud@Customer are to be explored for critical applications. Oracle Exadata is a converged architecture with compute, storage and networking all combined in an appliance with advanced technologies like hybrid columnar compression it is a key offering for massive database deployments with inbuilt HA and management modules. OCI is now on multicloud, public cloud, hybrid cloud and dedicated cloud. Thus oracle cloud is a major player in cloud.

In compute field it offers Flex VMs, Arm-based Compute, Bare Metal Servers, GPU-Accelerated Compute, HPC Compute and VMware. Oracle now offers new AI-powered OCI Search with OpenSearch 2.11. OCI now enables sovereign AI worldwide with Oracle's distributed cloud.

In Networking it offers Customer-Premises Equipment, DNS Management, FastConnect, Load Balancers, Networking Gateways, Private Endpoint, Site-to-Site VPN and Virtual Cloud Networks services.

In Application & Data integration it offers Service Oriented Architecture (SOA), GoldenGate, Autonomous Database Data Studio and Data Integrator. GoldenGate is a very powerful Data integration service from Oracle.

As Open Source Databases HeatWave MySQL is a fully managed database service, driven by integrated HeatWave in-memory query accelerator. As per Oracle It's the only cloud database service combining transactions, analytics, and ML services in one Database, delivering real-time and secure analytics without complexity,latency and cost of ETL duplication. It needs to be explored.

In Analytics and BI space OCI offers Oracle Analytics Platform, Oracle Fusion CX Analytics, Oracle Fusion ERP Analytics,Oracle Fusion HCM Analytics and Oracle Analytics mobile app.

In Storage technologies it addresses key use cases with on-demand local, object,file, block and archive storage. The services offered are Archive Storage, Block Volumes, Data Transfer Service, File Storage, Object Storage and Storage Gateway.

In Containers and Functions area it helps deploy microservices applications on high-performance, managed and open source based Docker, Kubernetes, and Fn Functions services. Services offered in this key area of modernization are Container Instances, Functions, Kubernetes Engine, Registry and Service Mesh.

Oracle Goldengate is a powerful and proven migration tool for migration of large databases taking care of tight cutover schedules.

# Oracle Goldengate Logical Architecture

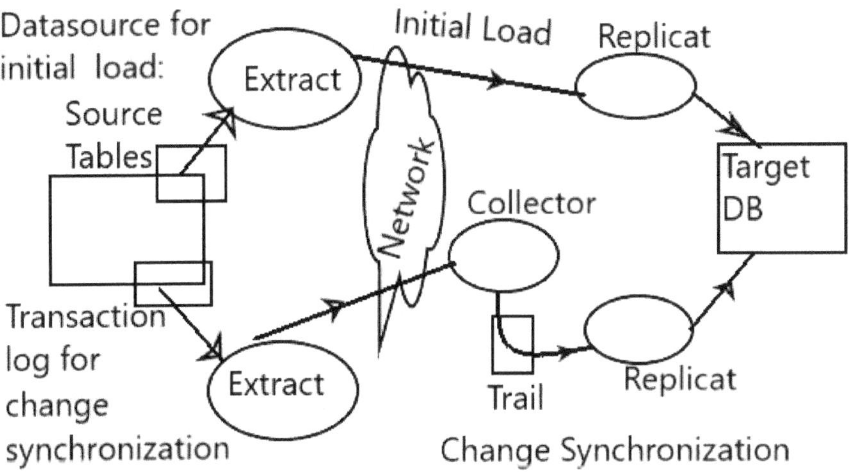


# A handy migration tool from Oracle

Oracle Dataguard is a proven and powerful tool for migration of critical and massive oracle clustered and non-clustered databases. The Dataguard can be logical, physical or snapshot standby. A standby database can easily be a primary database after planned failover or switchover. More than dozens of time I have seen multi terabyte databases to transition database role as often as required. A snapshot standby further enhances this capability by moving the transition marker quite elegantly with additional tests for accuracy of data. With a seasoned database architect around, and a good network connecting source and target, the cutover can be easily done for critical databases. Small and development databases can go for datapump.

Source: https://docs.oracle.com

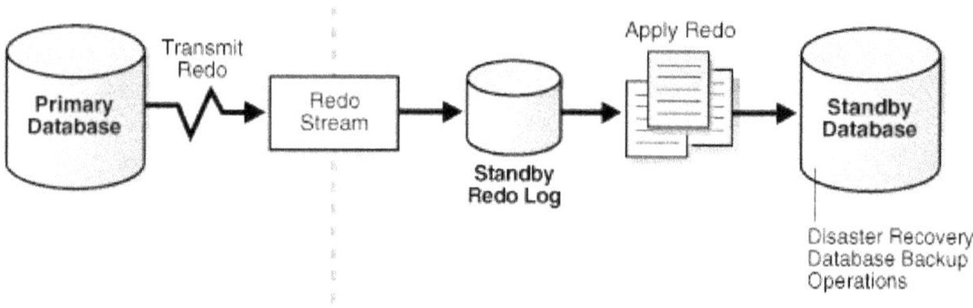


As per Oracle, Database 23c, is now generally available on OCI.

# Part II

Each customer's cloud migration strategy is different from others. Migration can be cloud to cloud, On-prem to cloud. Without proper understanding of the source applications and infrastructures in terms of capacity, development, integration and operations, migration can be risky and longer than expected.

# CHAPTER SEVEN

# ABC CORPORATE

Every IT organization now needs resources with cloud skills. Entry level skills is not enough to handle critical provisiong, deprovisiong, &management operations. Automating cloud provisioning using terraform is a much sought after skill nowadays. While different services requires different skills, some basic understanding of cloud is essential for employees to use cloud as a development or operation environment. As multi cloud and hybrid cloud is everywhere, it is also essential for advanced cloud engineers to acquire ability to integrate applications with more than one cloud. On cloud one can get various services which are globally used and available thus thought to adoption is no more a long journey. Developer's productivity increases with increase with choices of softwares. One can also use cloud marketplaces where several handy tools are added by trusted third party partners. License management is eased in cloud.

Cloud is not replacing the current skills. It is complementing and supplementing the current skill level in computing, storage, middlewares, networking, operations and managements. Cloud is primarily built around virtualization, kubernetis and evolution of internet computing. All the legacy data centres have either migrated to cloud or are migrating to cloud. Workforce can be anywhere and resources can be anywhere. Mobile & edge computing has taken cloud everywhere. CDN takes internet content distibution to everywhere around the globe. Bigdata and analytics has changed a lot. In a second thousands of computing resources can come up and start computing the massive workload in parallel and when not needed these computing resources can be shutdown. Thus many research areas can utilise this feature of cloud and bring rapid advances in research. From healthcare to space research cloud is utilised.

Public clouds are self served and this makes adoption of cloud easier. On major public cloud there is a vpc or virtual private cloud for deployment of critical workloads which requires dedicated resources. Every cloud has a backbone network built around WAN providers and all regional cloud DCs or POPS are connected around the backbone. Cloud segregates public, private, & management traffic using frontend and backend routers. SDDC, SD-WAN, Hypervisors, K8s make cloud less costly and flexible to operate. The skills on virtualization and K8s is in top demand apart from bigdata and AI skills.

Let us briefly go through the existing application deployment structure of an example software service unit of a corporate on one cloud and how it plans to move to another cloud.

1.Containerised Applications using OCP deployed on IBM Cloud.

1.1. Github enterprise for SCM

1.2. Jfrog for code repository

1.3. CI/CD using Redhat ArgoCD

1.4. Applications & Frameworks

1.4.1. KAFKA for message brokers

1.4.2. AAP & HUB for Automation

1.4.3. 3SCALE & SRA

1.4.4. Reporting & Monitoring.

1.4.5. Binary distribution service using Nexus

1.4.6. ABC App using Ruby for netcool integration

1.4.7. A File Service app for Patch scan repository

1.4.8. Inventory Producers

1.4.9. Backup

If the organization unit decides to move to Azure say, then it needs to assess the target cloud by conducting some PoC and benchmarking. The current challenges and drivers for cloud journey can be:

1-Cost optimization

2-SRE for HA and DR posture improvements

3-Monitoring enhancements

4-Manageability and governance

5-Opensource exploration

6-Modernization and transformation

Now it engages in POCs and Benchmarks for deciding a migration process in this Cloud to Cloud journey. If it decides to go for sevaral cloud native services and platforms, it needs to carry out several rounds of PoCs on the chosen services in target cloud.

Target cloud services and platforms chosen:

1-PaaS (ARO) as application deployment platforms.

2-Azure Cloud Native Services adoption

2.1.Postgres flexible server
2.2.Mysql server
2.3.Azure redis cache

3-SD WAN on Azure
4-AIOPS services
7-Sciencelogic integration
8-Splunk integration
9-Azure object storage
10-Azure API Manager

# CHAPTER EIGHT

# Cloud Journey of ABC

ABC corporate starts its cloud journey with discussions involving architecture, operations, management ,development and customer teams. Some questions to get started are given below. Answers should be collected and analyzed for future stages.

Which services are offered by which clouds?

Which services and features from which clouds match the desired future state?

What is the biggest challenge in the cloud journey?

In what order source workloads should be migrated to cloud?

What are the inter dependencies among source applications in terms of hardware and softwares?

Which workload needs which type of migration approach?

Estimating current and future capacity requirements of workloads?

Which network offerings of which cloud closely match the network bandwith, cutover schedules, cost expectation and skill level of source resources?

Is cloud being targeted for offloading backup requirements?

How quickly and easily the current applications in source can be transformed to microservices?

What is size of data migration needed and what coutover windows are acceptable?

What is the current operational and development challenges to be addressed in cloud?

What is the current HA and DR challenges to be addressed in target cloud?

Are the migration tools acceptable in terms of security standards of the organization?

What are the different migration tools available in different clouds?

Are the skill levels of current work force capable enough to handle migration challenges and what supports the target cloud teams can extend? The technical skill areas are network, storage, middlewares, applications, computing, virtualization, kubernetes, databases, IAM, monitoring etc. All the skills should be assessed and upgraded whereever necessary to handle cloud migration and post migration operations.

How are the out-of-support hardwares and softwares handled during migration? A current software and hardware catalog is needed to be created and validated against supported migration tools.

How are IP conflicts between source data centres and target data centres to be handled?

How are existing customer connectivity to be addressed from cloud?

Whether to optimize workload first and then migrate, or migrate workload first and upgrade later?

Which tools are used for discovery of existing applications as application discovery can be challenging?

Some applications may be frequently accessed. Some applications may be quite old and very rarely accessed and change management records may not be accurate to find all the active and necessary application sets.

How to engage with application users in terms of their future operational and availability needs?

Imagine a corporate has 30 data centres spread across globe, and each data centre has different workloads.

What is the approach to discover and categorize the workloads? What is the approach to estimate accurate cpu, storage, memory, and network capacity of workloads in target cloud? What is the accurate cpu, storage, memory, and network capacity of workloads in source on-premise data centre or cloud? How can the migration team handle out-of-support hardwares, softwares and firmwares? Where are the change logs to the resources located? Are all the source systems patched to the latest software updates? In what order the workloads are to be migrated? What integration challenges are expected in target cloud? Has the corporate adequate cloud skills to manage the migration, assuming cutover schedules are very tight in terms of business down time? How are the licences to be handled?

Some example workloads:

Websphere Servers
Weblogic Servers
Tomcat Apache Servers
Microsoft IIS Servers
Microsoft Domain Controllers
Developer Tools
Service Now Systemsi
Kafka Servers
Redhat Linux VMs
Solaris VMs
Windows VMs
IBM Power Servers
AIX VMs
VMware ESX servers
Oracle Sparc servers
IBM SANs
VMware VSANs
NAS Systems
Redhat OCPs
Cisco Switches and Routers
F5 LBRs
SAP HANA Systems
Vyatta Gateways
Fortinet FWs
Juniper vSRX Gateways
Physical Tape Libraries for Oracle Backup and Recovery
Exadata Appliances
Oracle RAC databases with ASM
MySQL Databases
Oracle Databases
DB2 Databases
Microsoft SQL Servers
Postgres Databases
Oracle Datawarehouses
Oracle CRM Systems
Oracle Apps
Peoplesoft Systems

The list can be huge. Some tasks that need to be carried out for a smooth migration:

1-Clear understanding of the current workloads and the future expectations.

2-Deciding a cloud and a deployment model to match the organization's short term and long term needs.

3-Assessing integration challenges with target cloud services.

4-Migration readiness review.

5-Data security review of the new deployment model.

6-Developing cloud skills for both during migration and post migration activities.

7-License & cost estimation of services in new environment.

8-Cloud account setup & test provisioning for PoCs.

9-PoCs for all SaaS, PaaS & IaaS services in the scope of migration.

10-Performance benchmarking of new services.

11-Architecture review board's approval once PoC and benchmarking results are in place.

12-Final migration planning & cutover schedules.

13-Monitoring and support structure in new environment.

What are some challenges in migration?

Lines of business (LOB) can't accurately predict migration costs.

Migrations are slow and inefficient because IT staff lacks the right skills or have no bandwidth.

Migrations are affected by a lack of a standard, consistent, and globally available discovery, planning and migration method.

Uncontrolled change management during migration impacts business during frequent down time.

Source IPs conflict with target IPs.

IPs are embedded in applications instead of FQDN(fully qualified domain name) making it difficult to detect during migration.

Lack of current state application architecture documents.

Mismatch of number and types of assets between configuration management databases and discovered applications.

Expired Certificates.

What all features are desired of a robust and reliable migration service?

Flexible: Flexible, predictable and market competitive.

Agile: Adaptable to desired pace of migration and transformation.

Consistent: Outcome of each task should be repeatable and not unexpected.

Comprehensive: It should be robust and cover all kinds of migration scenarios like Physical to Virtual, Virtual to Virtual, Cloud to Cloud, and Data Center to Cloud.

Highly secure: Data movements should be properly encrypted either at rest or in motion as desired.

What are the different migration phases?

Discover:

Self service Discovery, Infrastructure discovery, Shared Services and Middleware Discovery, Application Assessment & Maintenance of Discovered assets.

Plan:

Project management, Technical governance, High Level Events Planning, Detailed Event Planning.

Design and Build:

Infrastructure Design, Cloud Design, Migration Design, Application Profiling, Physical Build, Logical Build and Cloud Build.

Migrate:

Pre-migration Event Preparation, Migration Event Preparation, Migration Event Execution, Event Incident Management.

Test:

Build Verification, Pre-migration Testing, Migration Testing, and Post Migration Testing.

What are the different levels of migration and what all tools can be used to execute migration?

Some examples are given. Many tools and services are available in cloud and can be evaluated.

1-OS Image Transfer.

2-Database Migration.

3-Storage Migration.

Storage Level Migration:

Some Tools: CirrusData & Native SAN Migration Tools.

Source: FC SAN -> Target: FC SAN

VM Level Migration:

Some DB Migration Tools: AWS DMS, and DB Native Tools.

Source: Public and Private Cloud, & Traditional DC -> Target: AWS RDS, & DB on VM.

Host Migration Tools: Rackware, Zerto, Double-Take, and PLATESPIN etc. to name a few.

Source: Public and Private Cloud, & Traditional DC -> Target: Private & Public Cloud.

Cloud Native Tools: AWS SMS, & Azure Site Recovery.

Source: Public and Private Cloud, & Traditional DC -> Target: EC2 & Microsoft Azure.

Approaches: Migration should be performed as an ongoing activity and not as an all at once activity.

**Velostrata:** There are many tools and services from many vendors to assist in migration to cloud. One such tool is Velostrata which is used for lift and shift of VM using a vCentre plugin. It is a cloud migration tool acquired by Google to help customers shift theirs workloads to Google Cloud Platform (GCP). A Velostrata OnPrem virtual appliance is deployed in source virtual data center, and Velostrata Edge virtual appliance called cloud extension runs on target cloud.

Cirrus Data's Cirrus Migrate On-Premises (CMO) and Cirrus Migrate Cloud (CMC) help migrate any block storage in any location to any other block storage. The any-to-any feature of data mobility solutions is very helpful. Whether the new block storage is on-prem, in public cloud, or in a hybrid environment, customers can migrate data live with minimal or zero downtime, including cutover window. It is a partner with major clouds providers like Azure, Oracle, Google, and AWS etc.

CLOUD MIGRATION SOLUTIONS ARE:

1-CLOUD-TO-CLOUD MIGRATION.

2-ON-PREMISE-TO-CLOUD MIGRATION.

3-WITHIN-THE-CLOUD MIGRATION.

It has partnered with different vendors like Dell, Netapp, purestorage, HP etc. Cirrus Data helps in migration of any block workload to block-based storage on any Dell platform, including PowerFlex on-prem or in the cloud.

**Source: https://www.cirrusdata.com/success-stories-financial-6/**

There is a good success story for storage migration from EMC VNX to HPE 3PAR.

CHALLENGES:

• No downtime available until months after migration deadline.

• Limited information on existing environment.

• No changes to the source VNX storage were allowed due to known risks.

• Short implementation timeframe.

SOLUTION:

• CMO was inserted into path totally transparent to the hosts, FC switches, and the VNX storage.

• CMO auto-discovered all hosts, source LUNS, and paths.

• Maintained compatibility with PowerPath even after pMotion and I/O were going solely to the 3PAR array.

• Maintained compatibility for boot from SAN.

RESULTS:

• Eliminated risk of changes and application outage that are usually associated with using standard migration tools (host or appliance).

• Delivered on-time migration with predictability with full control over infrastructure and migration process.

• pMotion allows old storage to be removed without affecting the host by emulating the old storage using the new storage.

• No dependencies on other software, OS, storage array, applications versioning, or SAN array changes—allowed the migration to move forward without requiring remediation until final cutover.

Scope and imortance of of PoC: Whereever possible, E2E testing should be carried across the application stack. While a big corporate can survive several migration failures, just one failover and a startup or mid sized organization is gone. So, there should be some restraint in moving to cloud unless it is absolutely needed. Point is cloud adoption should be planned. With heavily priced storage and baremetal servers low latency can be achieved. But, with a careful database selection, even with a low cost open source database same or better low latency could have been achieved. People in architecture may not always understand the depth of critical software stacks and with over confidence can make migration slow. Careful evaluation of key architectual skills is needed for crucial migrations as business planners and executivies often have less bandwidth to assess all possible failure cases. Sometimes, there are dead lines to vacate old data centres, and in utter desperation organization units rush to cloud. After the initial euophria is over, old customers may find the same application behaving slow due to improper selection of DC location and tools. A broad and deep understanding is required to foresee the future behaviour of applications to a great extent. With many analytical tools on observing resource capacity behaviour, it is not so difficult to carry out proper benchmarking of source applications if not already done, or the application and infrastructure benchmarks were carried out long back without any relevance in the current load and usage scenario. Time may be the biggest factor to consider while planning. I have seen many migrations don't move ahead from requirements gathering phase and subsequent phases suffer with unknow data. While the CMDBs may be old and inaccurate, the tools to gather or discover applications may be inappropriate. AWS has a good set of tools for migration. There are tools for containerization as well. So, all the tools should be tested quickly giving oppertunity to arrive at fast decisions.

IaC: Terraform is a powerful tool for automated provisioning of cloud native services like Postgres flexible server, Azure redis cache, MYSQL server, VM, ARO, Vnet etc. Devops teams are increasingly using terraform based deployment to quickly deploy complex solutions involving many services in a predictable manner. Once the code is ready for consumption, it can be placed in oraganization's github for consumers to easily use the IaC to deploy the resources in as many instances as required. With CI/CD pipelines integrated in the Devops practices, the incremental release specific changes to IaC by Devops teams automatically get redeployed to target environments.

Automation, cloud, & AI are everywhere. And, enterprise Devops practices are rapidly switching to cloud to consume open source softwares and cloud native services for easier management, monitoring and reduction of cost. Job cut is real and competion in IT is fierce. And, there is no going back to older technologies. Point is, cloud journey is everwhere. Some are beginning to start, some are mid-way, while many are already on cloud.

# Part III

A deep understanding of cloud native architecture, capability of different hypervisors, core of container computing, ACID properties of Databases, NoSQL database capabilities, Networking stacks and protocols, SAN, NAS etc. are key to handling a successful migration and future modernization and transformation drives. Different Clouds offer different migration tools and each selected tool needs a PoC to validate its promised functionalites in the context of this instance of migration. Each customer environment is different from others and each migration is in someway or the other different from other similar migration cases with other customers in terms of network bandwidth, cutover schedules, source application types and versions, source location, data sizes and skills of resources involved. New bugs may surface and delay the migration schedules. Test PoC network environment incurs additional cost during test migrations and may not match the accurate capacity and bandwidth requirement due to improper source capacity estimation.

# CHAPTER NINE

# BAREMETAL AND K8S

Some key skill areas are VMware and K8s. For example, how vMotion works.

Live Migration of Virtual Machines using vMotion and Storage vMotion. Hosts can be in different geography.

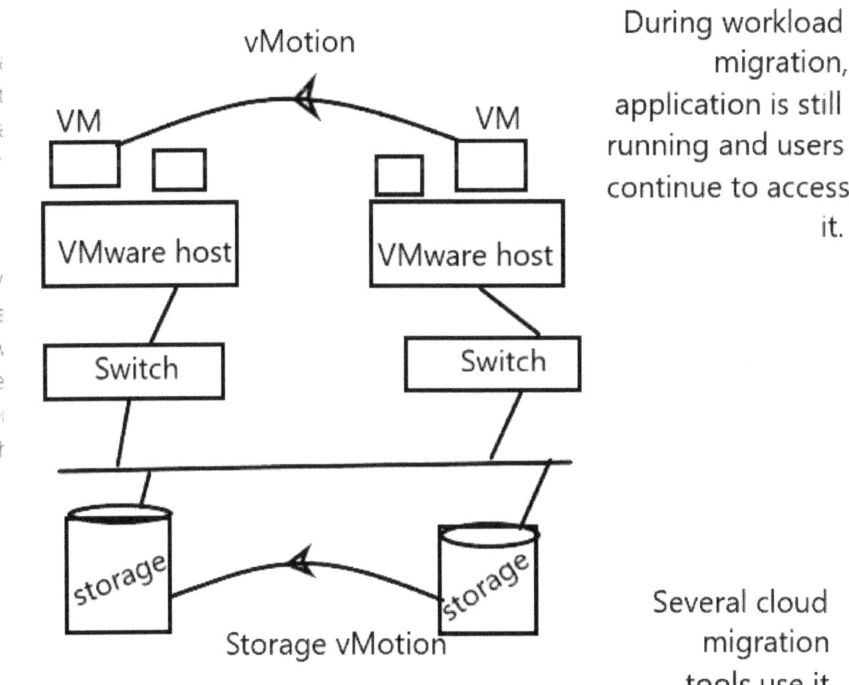


During workload migration, application is still running and users continue to access it.

Several cloud migration tools use it.

**Source: https://www.virtualizationworks.com**

What is VMware HCX?

VMware HCX®, an application mobility platform, simplifies application migration, workload rebalancing, and business continuity across data centers and clouds. VMware HCX enables high-performance, large-scale app mobility across VMware vSphere® and non-vSphere cloud and on-premises environments to accelerate data center modernization and cloud transformation. VMware HCX automates the creation of an optimized network interconnect and extension, and facilitates interoperability across KVM, Hyper-V and vSphere 6.0+ to current vSphere versions. This delivers live and bulk migration capabilities without redesigning the application or re-architecting networks.

K8s skill is very crucial. OCP, ROSA, ARO etc. are critical K8s platforms for microservice deployments. This expample gives a high level view of an ARO(Azure Redhat Openshift) cluster architecture in only internal LB mode. Express route helps connect to this cluster from On-prem. Over service end points the cluster accesses essential services like container registry. Customers needing a suitable microservice platform for modernization and transformation of workloads can evaluate this platform. ARO provides many operators out-of-the-box like ArgoCD (for CI/CD pipelines), 3Scale (for API management), Nexus (for binary distribution service).

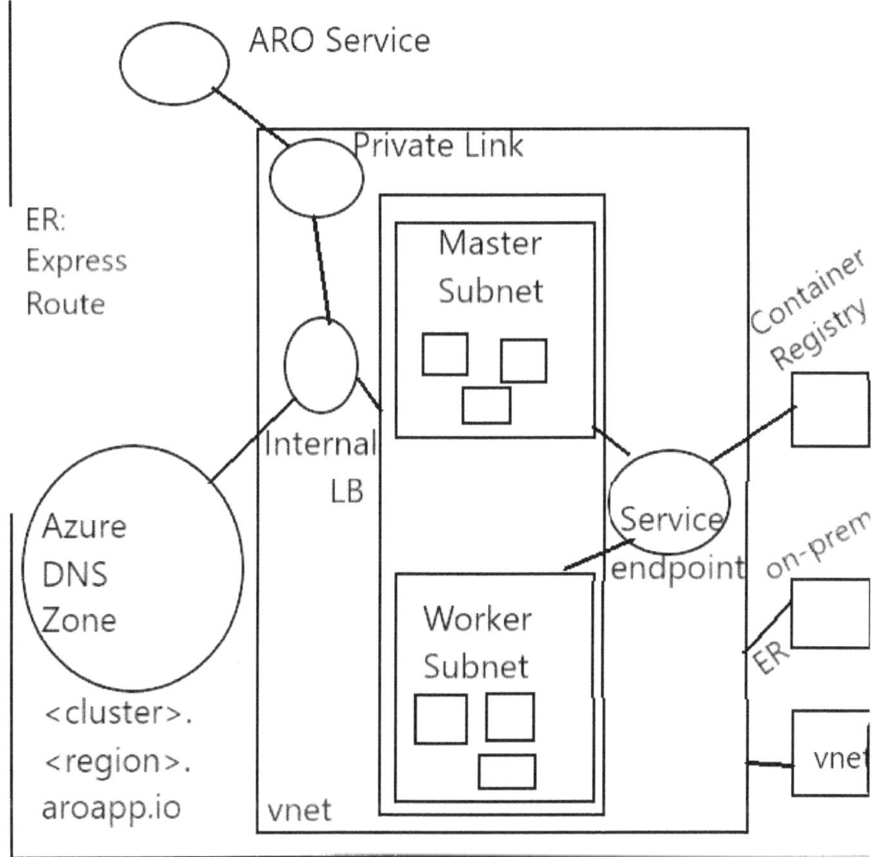


Some basic assignements can be tryed to see how a containerised application serves request.

1-Login to aro from CLI using oc on an account jump host.

2-Create a namespace in aro.

3-Deploy an application in aro cluster.

4-Check the pods constituting the application are up and running.

5-Login to application from a browser on an account jump host.

Some basic examples can be checked from (Source: https://nordcloud.com/blog/getting-started-with-aro-application-deployment/)

Some basic ARO commands used by ARO admins.

    oc login
oc get nodes
oc get projects
oc get sc
oc get routes
oc get services
oc get pvc
oc get pv

Lets check what is there in a container in a pod in a project or application in an ARO K8s cluster.

```
[me@vmwusxyz ~]$ oc get pods
NAME                             READY     STATUS    RESTARTS  AGE
 podxxx   .                       3/3      Running   0         36h
```

So,. the pod above has 3 containers. What are they?

```
kubectl get pods podxxx  -o jsonpath='{.spec.containers[*].name}'

cp-kafka-broker    prometheus-jmx-exporter     vault-agent
```

Let us rsh into a container of the pod.

```
$ oc rsh -c prometheus-jmx-exporter podxxx
# df
Filesystem      1K-blocks         Used Available    Use% Mounted on
overlay         1073206252 153267552 919938700  15%  /
```

# CHAPTER TEN

# KEY DATABASE TECHNOLOGIES

Dataops covers collection, transformation, movement, storage, archival and retrieval of data. The sources can be databases, IOT devices, batch processes all spread across the globe. Data can be structured, unstructured and semi structured. Movement of data through data pipelines across the globe and across enterprises in a fast and secure manner is a challenge for many organizations. Size of data is on the rise as huge unstructured data from different social media platforms too get integrated with data from main stream business operations. Whether to go for ETL or ELT too is a critical decision. AI or generative AI all need accuracy of data. Fast and secure data retrieval and loading often is a challenge. Data migration during cloud migration is a crucial step in large scale data migration poc and cutover excercises. Data can be stored in databases or object storages. Different clouds offer different ways for analytics operations. And careful analysis of different bigdata and analytics offerings requires crucial skills. Arriving at proper type of databases during migration is a crucial decision to cater to the need of a few milli or sub milli seconds latency in data access.

Lets have a brief overview of different databases offered by different vendors.

Data warehouses, data marts, and data lakes are all getting transformed or modernized as part of cloud migration to exploit massive integration opertunities with rich and open source based cloud native tools and services.

Critical RDBMS like Oracle and DB2 are moving to cloud along with critical hypervisor and kubernetis platforms. And migrating data of huge oracle databases from legacy data centres to clouds like google,IBM,Azure and AWS is no easy operations. Appliances and fast interconnects are often used around edge locations to meet tight cutover schedules for critical databases.

ACID properties of databases get redefined with distributed data storage using distributed databases and hadoop systems. Both horizontal and vertical scalings can be evaluated along with data consistency requirements.

While open source databases can be used whereever possible evaluating the needs of business is of paramount importance. What is the value of migrating to open source vendors if business needs are not met?

So, cloud adoption should be strategically evaluated. A key concept to understand is the difference between SQL DBs and NoSQL DBs.

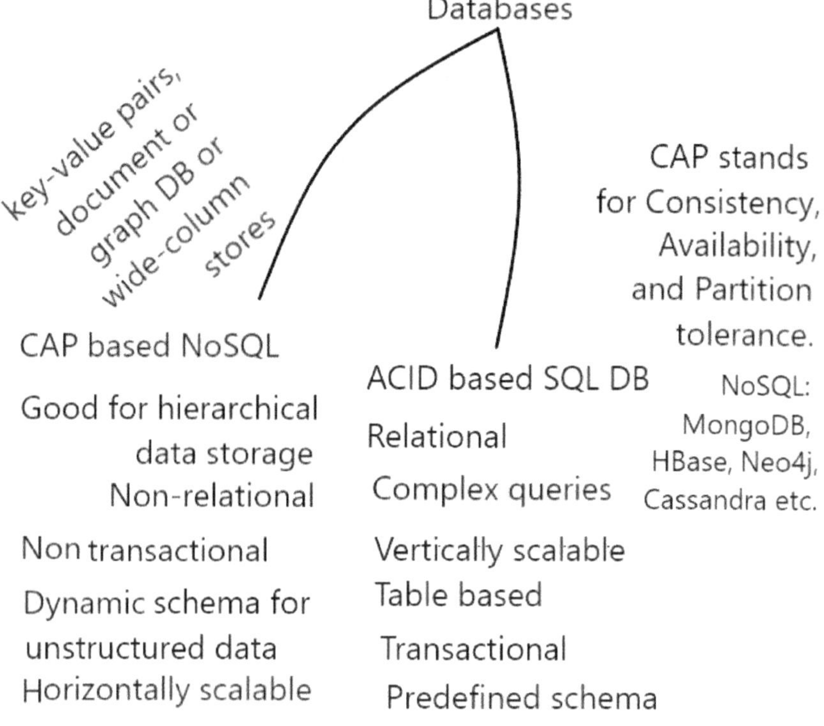


While Hadoop cluster is a set of data nodes with shards supporting hive query, Cassandra is a popular NoSQL database. Here are some interesting comparisions.

| Hadoop | Cassandra |
| --- | --- |
| Batch processing | Real time processing |
| Master slave architecture | Distributed |
| Map reduce | Cassandra QL |
| File compression around 10-15% | Upto 80% |
| Indexing is difficult | Indexing is easy |
| Uses HDFS system | Uses keyspace column family concept |
| Replication factor is 3 | No of nodes in cluster |
| Data protection uses RPC and Datagram protocol | Data protection with commit log design |

# CHAPTER ELEVEN

# BASICS OF NETWORK OS AND SAN

IT infrastructure services are broadly categorized into computing, storage and networking. Computing tier can be baremetal or physical devices or virtual machines based on hypervisors. Computing tier is further modernized as containers. Storage can be file, block or object based. WAN can be MPLS based or Software defined. Network components like routers, switches, load balancers, gateways etc. are all being software defined. Virtualization and containerization has changed the tools and components in software industry in a massive way. Monolithic applications and hardware systems are modernized into smaller and flexible units. SAN and NAS systems too are getting software defined. Open source based cloud native services running on containers is transforming application systems and are adopted hugely. While basic os concepts like memory management, process structure, process scheduling, input or output device management etc. remains the same the behaviour and speed of io drivers depend on type of virtualization. When multi tenancy is choosen, on one baremetal there can be many vms used by many customers in a shared manner. So the workload redistribution in cloud should be carefully analyzed by experts to get similar or better response times for applications deployed on cloud. Any change in hypervisors from source to target should be properly tested.

# CHAPTER TWELVE

# COMMON QUESTIONS

Q3. What are some of the key features of Cloud Computing?

Some key features are:

Scalable: Cloud computing allows the resources to auto scale up and down when needed. Auto scaling groups can be configured, so when consumption goes down number of resources like vms can be reduced and when consumption again increases the number of vms automatically increase.

Agile: Cloud services can be quickly provisioned, enabling the bussiness to respond rapidly to demands.

Location independence: The user can access cloud services from anywhere anytime with an internet connection. This increases flexibility in work environment and results in enhanced productivity.

Multitenant: Cloud providers can serve many users or accounts on shared infrastructure, improving resource utilization and delivering services at less cost.

Dedicated: When consistent computing power is required for some critical applications, Baremetal servers can be provisioned.

Reliable: Cloud services are designed with redundancy and backup, providing high availability and DR without significant efforts in building and testing these solutions. DR drills are reduced.

Metered usage: Cloud services can be billed either monthly or hourly as per need. Google offers even per second billing for certain services.

Q5. What are some of the cloud service models?

There are various cloud service models, such as:

IaaS: It offers computing resources like servers, storage, and networking over the internet, giving users control over their own operating systems and applications.

PaaS: It provides a prebuilt platform with tools for developing, hosting, and deploying applications without the need to build and manage the underlying infrastructure.

FaaS: It allows developers to run code in response to events, paying only for the actual usage of resources.

SaaS: It delivers complete software systems, without the need to install and configure the software.

Anything-as-a-Service or XaaS: It is used for cloud services which provide special solutions like DBaaS expanding the "as-a-Service" model.

What are some Cloud Storage Levels? They are block, file and object.

What is meant by edge computing?

It brings computing closer to the source data thus reducing unnecessary data movements and improving response times.

What is cloud native application or cloud native architecture?

CNA is a software framework leveraging K8s and containers to build microservice based applications. This reduces cost of deployment and makes application behave consistently irrespective of the underlying hardware and OS. It is a major driver for cloud adoption. Microservice oriented architecture means the monolithic and difficult to manage application is decomposed into modular, independent services that interact through well-defined service contracts. Containerized applications are light in nature and can be quickly scaled up and down quite easily. Container packaging enables densely packed applications.

What are the building blocks of cloud architecture?

The building blocks of cloud architecture are technical architecture, reference architecture etc.